Ghost Stories

Compilation of horrifyingly REAL ghost stories-

Truly disturbing-Hauntings & Paranormal stories

By Hannah J. Tidy

Hannah J. Tidy

© Copyright 2017 -Night Terror Publishing All rights reserved.

In no way is it legal to reproduce, duplicate, or transmit any part of this document in either electronic means or in printed format. Recording of this publication is strictly prohibited, and any storage of this document is not allowed unless with written permission from the publisher. All rights reserved.

The information provided herein is stated to be truthful and consistent, in that any liability, in terms of inattention or otherwise, by any usage or abuse of any policies, processes, or directions contained within is the solitary and utter responsibility of the recipient reader. Under no circumstances will any legal responsibility or blame be held against the publisher for any reparation, damages, or monetary loss due to the information herein, either directly or indirectly.

Respective authors own all copyrights not held by the publisher.

Hannah J. Tidy

Legal Notice:

This book is copyright protected. This is only for personal use. You cannot amend, distribute, sell, use, quote or paraphrase any part or the content within this book without the consent of the author or copyright owner. Legal action will be pursued if this is breached.

Disclaimer Notice:

Please note the information contained within this document is for educational and entertainment purposes only. Every attempt has been made to provide accurate, up to date and reliable, complete information. No warranties of any kind are expressed or implied. Readers acknowledge that the author is not engaging in the rendering of legal, financial, medical or professional advice.

By reading this document, the reader agrees that under no circumstances are we responsible for any losses, direct or indirect, which are incurred as a result of the use of information contained within this document, including, but not limited to, —errors, omissions, or inaccuracies.

Question! Do you like FREE books?

As a thank you for buying my book I would like to offer my other book for **FREE** The Scarcest Reddit stories: That turned out to be true!

Download it for **FREE** Here

>> www.nightterrorpublishing.com/book-club <<

In addition to getting The Scarcest Reddit stories: That turned out to be true! You will also have an opportunity to enter our Horror Book Club Newsletter where you can get

Hannah J. Tidy

FREE Horror books sent conveniently to your inbox as well as FREE giveaway contests, and discounts!

In this Chilling compilation, you will discover some of the most horrifying ghost stories posted to Reddit, that turned out to be true. You won't believe what you are reading!

Ghost Stories

Table of Contents

Introduction 11

Chapter 1 Ghosts -Justice From Beyond The Greenbrier Ghost 15

Chapter -2 Ghosts- From Hallowed Halls to the Pages of a Magazine The Brown Lady of Raynham Hall 31

Chapter 3 Ghosts - Emails from the Other Side Jack Froese 47

Chapter 4 Ghosts- To Raise the Devil The Ghosts of Taunton State Hospital.. 55

Chapter 5 Paranormal - When Science Collides with the Paranormal The Possession of Julia 65

Chapter -6 Ghosts - Erzsébet Báthor The Real Queen Ravenna... 75

Chapter -7 Ghosts - The Winchester House The Never-Ending Construction.. 83

Chapter -8 Ghosts - The Flying Dutchman Lost At Sea 91

7

Hannah J. Tidy

Chapter -9 The Paris Catacombs Darkness Beneath the City of Light 97

Chapter -10 Hauntings - The Hands Resist Him Haunted eBay Painting 105

Chapter -11 Hauntings – Robert the Doll When Dolls Stop Being Toys 111

Chapter -12 Hauntings – Annabelle Another Hardly Amusing Toy 123

Chapter -13 Hauntings – Doris Bither The Horror behind the Horror 135

Chapter -14 Hauntings - The Cecil Hotel Elisa Lam Tapes And More 147

Chapter -15 Hauntings – Amityville The House of Terror 153

Chapter -16 Hauntings - Overtoun Bridge Gateway Between Worlds 167

Chapter -17 Paranormal - Jeffrey Dahmer Shape Shifting 173

Ghost Stories

Chapter -18 Paranormal – Cannock Chase The Black-Eyed Children..179

Chapter -19 Paranormal – Mount Washington Hotel The Carolyn Stickney EVP 189

Chapter -20 Paranormal – The Goldfield Hotel The Clearest EVP Ever Recorded? 201

Chapter -21 Paranormal - Natasha Demkina: X-Ray Vision 211

Conclusion...217

About The Author 221

Check Out my other books 223

Hannah J. Tidy

Introduction

Ghost stories have always been a part of human culture. They take shape in different forms throughout the world and even play key roles in the legends of many ancient civilizations. They have long been the subject of famous pieces of literature and appear in great literary works such as Emily Brontë's *Wuthering Heights*, Bram Stoker's *Dracula,* and William Shakespeare's *Hamlet.* But are these stories merely fiction? As with most myths, there is generally a seed of truth to be found. Take the legend of Dracula, for example. It is based on a real person called Vlad Tepes, a Romanian ruler in the 16th century who was infamously known for impaling his beaten enemies and prisoners of war with giant stakes. If you dare to read on, you may be amazed to find that real live ghost stories and paranormal activity have been proven as fact for many centuries.

But what exactly is a ghost, you might ask? The answer to that question is not all that simple, as different worldviews influence our belief in the spiritual world. Nowadays, many people do not believe that a spiritual world even exists. In general, however, those that do believe in ghosts classify them as the spirit or apparition of a person or animal that has died and is still haunting the world. They can appear as all kinds of forms, from translucent beings that appear merely as shadows floating in the air, to more concrete but still shadowy phantoms with particular faces or features.

Perhaps the most alluring aspect of the spiritual world is that it is something that is mysterious which cannot, until the present time, be fully explained. Even with all the modern technology at our disposal, there are still things in the realm of the supernatural that are beyond science and logic. Think about a secret that you have kept for a long time. What is more exciting, keeping a secret to provide a little more mystery, or actually revealing the secret? My guess is that you received more satisfaction out of pondering the mystery more than anything else. The same thing goes for ghosts, hauntings, and paranormal activity. If we could completely understand all of it, it would then lose its allure.

Ghost Stories

We will be looking at some of the most terrifying stories ever recorded and supported with hard evidence. Specifically, we will examine a few different examples of supernatural events in each of the following types of stories in this book: ghost stories, hauntings, and paranormal activity. These stories have been recorded all over the globe, and while the specific happenings listed here are not exclusive, they are a fair representation of the types of stories in existence.

Hannah J. Tidy

Chapter 1-
Ghosts -Justice From Beyond

The Greenbrier Ghost

The truth will come out one way or another. No matter how hard we try, it will always reveal itself. It may take time, in some cases centuries, but in the long run, the one thing you can never hide from is the truth. In the case of the Greenbrier Ghost, the world saw evidence of this. It was the paranormal that facilitated this coming out of the truth, and it was the ghost herself who managed to convict her murderer.

In the Greenbrier County of West Virginia, a young girl was murdered in 1897. After her body had been examined only partially, it was assumed she had died of natural causes. It was not until her spirit appeared and revealed the truth that the case was reopened and her killer found. It is said that she visited her mother in her dreams, and convinced her that she had been brutally choked to death, a fact that a proper autopsy would later confirm.

The story begins in the year 1873 when Elva Zona Heaster was born in Greenbrier County, West Virginia, in the United States of America. Her early life and childhood years remain a mystery to the general public, as we know very little about who she was or what she did. However, it is public record that she got pregnant when she was barely out of her teens and was a mother out of wedlock when she was 22 years old. The fate of the child remains unknown. In 1895, she and her family met with the man who would become her husband, and eventually, her murderer.

Ghost Stories

Edward Stribbling Trout Shue was a blacksmith and had just moved to Greenbrier County himself, in search of a better life. For Zona, who had been raised in the Richlands all of her life, he was a breath of fresh air that she had not encountered before. Shue, who worked at the shop of their usual blacksmith, attracted her attention almost immediately. After their initial meeting, Zona frequently returned to the shop to see him. Their romance was one of a Harlequin whirlwind affair. Barely a few months had passed before they were tying the knot and saying their wedding vows in church.

Zona's family, however, was not exactly pleased with their union. Her mother, in particular, was dead set against it. Mary Jane Heaster had taken a total, and instant dislike to the man her daughter had fallen in love with, and openly objected to their union. But there was little she could do, and in the end, Zona and her new husband began their life together in their little log house.

It only took three months before their marriage began to fall apart. Zona did not know it then, but she had essentially signed her life away to a serial offender, as there were things about her husband that she would never come to know. On the 23rd of January in 1897, Shue sent his neighbor's young boy to check in on his wife to see if she needed anything. He was going to the market, he claimed, and he wanted to see if she wanted him to get anything for her. The neighbor's boy did as he was told and walked into the Shue household, straight through the front door, only to find Zona's body lying at the foot of the stairs, lifeless.

For a long moment, the boy stood there, staring at her, because he had no idea what to do or even what was happening. He was only a child, after all. Who knows what kind of trauma he went through as he stumbled upon the dead body of Zona Heaster. Her body was positioned in a manner that seemed unnatural. She was stretched out straight, and her legs had been pulled together. One of her arms was stretched out across her chest while the other rested at her side, and her head was tilted. She actually looked like she was quietly sleeping. In fact, this was the first thought that went through the boy's head when he first saw her. Given that he was young and innocent and the area was not known for rampant crime, it was hardly surprising that

Ghost Stories

his first reaction was to assume that Zona was merely resting.

He stepped towards her lifeless body and called her name softly. When his quiet, "Mrs. Shue?" received no response, the realization sank in that something was seriously wrong. He panicked and raced out of the house, running straight to his mother telling her all he had seen. Fearful for the worst, the woman called for the local coroner, Mr. George W. Knapp.

Knapp, who also served as a doctor for the county, did not come to the Shue's house for almost an hour after he received the call. By the time he finally made it into the house, Shue himself had come back home and had carried his wife's body up the staircase and into their bedroom. He had laid her body out on their bed and dressed her up.

This activity was the first suspicious detail in the case. It was considered rather strange for a man to wash and prepare a body. That was deemed to be a woman's job. Shue claimed that he had wanted to prepare his wife for her burial and dressed her in a high-necked dress with a stiff collar. He also placed a veil over her face and refused to leave her dead body while Knapp came closer to examine it.

Knapp testified that Shue remained in the room during the entire time he was examining the corpse. He saw that Shue was terribly upset and pained at the loss of his wife. Not wanting to cause the man any more grief, he kept his examination short. He noted that there was some slight bruising around Zona's neck, but given that Shue was at that time holding her dead form close to him and sobbing over it, he did not make a big deal out of it. Shue also reacted almost violently when Knapp attempted to get a closer look. He pounced on the doctor and became extremely agitated. Knapp did not want to aggravate him any further, and not having found any other signs of foul play, he simply left the house.

Knapp had also been treating Zona prior to her death. He originally listed the cause of death as an 'everlasting faint,' but later changed it to 'childbirth.' For close to two weeks before she died, she had been under treatment for what Knapp cited as 'female trouble,' though whether she was pregnant or not is something that has never been confirmed.

Ghost Stories

Perhaps she was trying to get pregnant and consulting with him for advice. For whatever the reason, Knapp, as her doctor, decided to go with childbirth as the cause of her death, and the case was closed. Her parents were informed of her passing and arrangements for her burial were made.

On the 24th of January in 1897, Zona Shue was buried in the local cemetery. Currently, the place still exists, and it is known as the Soule Chapel Methodist Cemetery. Interestingly, Zona's husband reacted a little too strongly during the burial itself. He showed utter devotion to his wife and was extremely protective of her body in a manner that came across as more of a psychotic killer than a grieving husband, a truth that would not come to light until much later. He kept close vigil over her; constantly hovering by the open casket, she was placed in and not allowing anyone else to come close to her - not even her parents. He would not let anyone touch her, especially when he put a pillow on the side of her head. His behavior was extremely erratic. His demeanor alternated between grieving loudly and painfully for his wife and suddenly becoming extremely energetic and delighted.

Apart from the pillow, he also placed a rolled up sheet on the other side of her head, cushioning her neck entirely so that it would not be visible. To add to that, he also tied a long scarf around her neck. The pillow and the sheet, he claimed tearfully, would aid his wife in her final rest and make it more comfortable. The scarf was her favorite item of clothing, and it was his farewell to her, even if it did not match the burial dress she was wearing. As they moved her to the cemetery, they noticed that her head was lolling about in a strangely loose manner. Shue was generally well-liked by the community and respected as a blacksmith, so he was not questioned, and all his strange behavior was chalked up to that of a grieving husband.

Zona's mother, Mary Jane Heaster, on the other hand, refused to believe that he was without any blame. She was convinced that he had done something to her daughter, though she had no proof. After the burial, she took the sheet from her daughter's body and handed it to her son-in-law, who refused to take it back. Confused, she took it home with her, where she noticed a strange smell on it.

Ghost Stories

Assuming that it was simply dirty or unclean, she washed it. This was when Zona's ghost made her first appearance. Physically, there was nothing wrong with the sheet, it was not as dirty as one might expect it to be and certainly did not warrant a full wash. Mrs. Heaster washed it anyways, and when she dropped the sheet into the basin, the water turned red.

One would assume that this was merely a red stain washing off. But what is interesting is that Mrs. Heaster saw the water's red color spread *onto* the sheet instead of the other way around. The color of the water stained into the sheet, turning it red while the *water* became clear. No matter how hard Mrs. Heaster tried, she could not wash the red stain off the sheet. She was sure this was a clear indication that something was wrong and that Zona's spirit was communicating with her in a plea for help.

Skeptics would probably claim some scientific explanation for the entire process, but the fact remains that Mrs. Heaster was a believer. Already having suspected her son-in-law of foul play, she knew that this was a sign from her daughter herself. She took to praying every night, hoping for another

23

sign or a clue as to how to prove that her daughter had been murdered. She wanted justice, and she did not know how to get it.

For the next four weeks, she prayed. Every night, she would sit down and cry for her daughter to return and tell her the truth. Her faith was finally rewarded at the end of those four weeks when Zona appeared to her in a dream. The night was cold, and the air was fraught with tension when Zona appeared to Mrs. Heaster and told her the whole truth.

This is what Zona's ghost revealed. Shue was a man possessed of a cruel nature. He was prone to abusing the people closest to him and had regularly beat Zona. He often had violent fits, and that day, he flew into a rage when she told him that she had not made any meat for dinner. In his anger, he had snapped her neck, thus explaining the strange angle of her head and the looseness to her neck as the corpse was transported to the cemetery.

To prove that her neck was indeed broken, the ghost of her daughter turned her head around so that it was facing backward, and all Mrs. Heaster saw was a head of hair floating on top of her shoulders and body. It goes without

Ghost Stories

saying that she was frightened beyond her wits and woke up screaming, hardly able to believe what she had seen. She might have been a believer and had even been praying for the exact sign that she had just received, but a sight like that is enough to send chills down the spine of anyone!

She was inclined not to believe her dream, and ready to dismiss it as just another figment of the post-traumatic stress she had experienced, especially given the way the ghost's neck twisted completely around to bring her face back to the front. Over the course of the next four days, the dream would repeat itself. Mrs. Heaster reported that Zona appeared again and again. First, there would be a bright light that would shine behind her eyelids, and then slowly, a mist would solidify into her dead daughter's sunken corpse, the room becoming utterly cold and frigid. This went on until Mrs. Heaster finally realized that she had gotten the proof she needed to fight for justice for her murdered daughter.

She went to the local prosecutor, a man by the name of John Alfred Preston, to whom she tried to convince of her son-in-law's guilt. Obviously, with a ghost story as her only proof, he was hesitant to reopen the case. It is reported that she spent several hours with him in his study, arguing to convince him that her daughter did not die due to what was previously assumed. Zona was murdered and deserved justice. Whether he believed her story about her daughter's ghost or not, we do not know, but he did reopen the case, going on the belief that there was something suspicious about the whole situation. Noting that a few of the other local people had also stated that Shue was acting strangely, Preston considered that perhaps Zona's death had not been as innocent as it appeared.

Preston went to interview people that had been involved with the case. The first of the witnesses to be interviewed was Dr. Knapp, who revealed that his examination of the body had been incomplete at best and that he had not done a proper autopsy. Preston ordered for the body to be exhumed and that an autopsy be conducted. An inquest jury was also formed to look into the death, and it was slowly turning into an investigation, not just a tragedy.

This is where skeptics would have to accept the truth because the autopsy confirmed what Mrs. Heaster had already known. Up until then, it was possible to have

Ghost Stories

dismissed her dreams and the appearance of her daughter's ghost as something triggered by loss and psychosis. However, medical evidence proved that whatever she 'dreamed' was completely right. Her daughter told her how she had been killed, and the autopsy confirmed it.

Zona's body was exhumed and put under examination on the 22nd of February, 1897. The autopsy went on for close to three hours, and they found that her neck had, indeed, been snapped, just as the ghost had pointed out. The windpipe was smashed in, and she was choked to death, as the marks of fingers on her neck proved. The neck had become dislocated between the first two vertebrae. That Mrs. Heaster could have dreamed up in such detail, the details of her daughter's death are highly unlikely. Zona wanted justice for what was done to her, and she appealed to her mother to get it.

Zona's husband, Shue, complained about his wife's body being exhumed. He told his friends that he knew he was going to be taken into custody, but he was confident of escaping since there was no real evidence of his guilt. As he predicted, the police arrested him once the autopsy was complete and he was sent to the jail in Lewisburg to await his trial.

It was during this time that the truth about him came to light. His name was not Edward, as he had claimed, but Erasmus. He was from Augusta County, and he had been married two times before he met Zona. His first wife took their daughter and left him when he went to jail for stealing. She later told the police that he had been abusive during their marriage. His second wife died barely a year after they were married, with no particular reason being cited.

While in jail in Lewisburg, Shue boasted that he wanted to marry seven women. Everything pointed to him being a serial abuser and killer. He was strangely confident of getting away with his crimes since there was very little evidence to prove his wrongdoing. The trial began in June 1897, with Mrs. Heaster as Preston's star witness. Preston, as an experienced attorney, knew that the idea of her daughter's ghost would not give her credibility. He limited his questions to the known facts, expertly avoiding the ghost sightings and focusing on the truth.

Ghost Stories

The truth was that it was Zona's appearance that had instigated the entire trial in the first place, and Mrs. Heaster was a believer. Shue's lawyer attempted to discredit her during his cross-examination by trying to prove her as a liar and a cheat. Mrs. Heaster, however, knew what she had seen. She staunchly defended her belief, and despite clear badgering, she would not go retract what she said. In lawyer terms, it was the defense that had taken up the issue of the ghost. This meant that the judge could not instruct the jury to disregard the testimony, and they had to either believe or disbelieve what was said based on their own impressions. Since their impressions were formed on the truth that Zona's spirit had come back from the dead asking for justice, they could not deny Mrs. Heaster's testimony.

Shue was found guilty of her murder and then sentenced to life in prison. A lynch mob formed to hang him for his crimes, but they were stopped, and he was sent to jail instead. He was sentenced to the West Virginia State Penitentiary, located in Moundsville. He lived there for three years before he passed away in March 1900 from an unknown illness. He was buried in the local graveyard.

29

For the rest of her life, Mrs. Heaster never recanted the story of her daughter's ghost as many skeptics expected her to. She received justice, so why would she continue lying? This was what skeptics advocated. However, the truth was that she *had* seen her daughter and the paranormal incident *had* instigated the trial. Zona's ghost was never heard from again. Her mother died, having never seen Zona again after the triumphant end of the trial. Whether the ghost actually appeared to her or not, there definitely was something extraordinary happening that could not be denied.

The State could not deny it either. A historical marker made of stone has been erected and set up near the cemetery that Zona is buried in. It reads:

Interred in nearby cemetery is Zona Heaster Shue. Her death in 1897 was presumed natural until her spirit appeared to her mother to describe how her husband Edward killed her. Autopsy on the exhumed body verified the apparition's account. Edward, found guilty of murder, was sentenced to the state prison. Only known case in which testimony from a ghost helped convict a murderer.

(Credit – Wikipedia and Google)

Chapter -2

Ghosts- From Hallowed Halls to the Pages of a Magazine

The Brown Lady of Raynham Hall

When you retreat to a peaceful and serene country house in England, you would expect the experience to be calm and relaxing. The last thing you would expect is to come face to face with a ghost. And yet, this is precisely what the visitors to Raynham Hall experience when they go to stay at the place. The Brown Lady of Raynham Hall is quite the infamous ghost, having been sighted a number of times over the years, going so far as to have been photographed and published in a magazine!

Raynham Hall is a country house in Norfolk, England. It has been and still is, with the Townshend family for close to a period of four centuries. The Hall lent its name to the five nearby estate villages, collectively known as The Raynhams', and was the backdrop for the infamous photo of the Brown Lady of Raynham Hall published in the *Country Life* magazine in 1936.

The manor is one of the most beautiful and splendid buildings in the Norfolk area. Its construction began in 1619, but it ended up being a false start, resulting in nothing but the collection of a significant amount of Ketton stone in the area until 1621. It wasn't until 1622 that the actual construction began. By the time the owner, Sir Roger Townshend, passed away in 1637, it was almost entirely finished. However, the manor remained unfurnished as some rooms were not fitted out and would not be completed in full until much later.

It was not until the second Viscount, Charles Townshend, that the manor would be vaulted into infamy. William Kent, one of Britain's most lauded and sought after architects and designers of that era, worked for Charles Townshend to construct additions and extensions to the manor's interior. His style is notably seen in the North Front of the manor, which he aligned closely with the work of the famous architect Inigo Jones. Between 1725 and 1732, Kent built the entire northern wing of the manor. He also decorated the interiors, bringing elements of his own personal style, evident in the aesthetically and architecturally pleasing carvings of the chimneypieces, in the doorways, and even the staircase that was painted to imitate niches.

To this day, if you walk into Raynham Hall, you can see the architect's style and his genius in designing the entire mansion. Not only did he design a structurally sound building, but he also gave the interiors a majestic touch, which the family reinforced by putting up paintings and portraits that would, in today's market, go for hundreds of thousands of dollars. In fact, some of these paintings are still in the mansion today, even after the auctions that took place in the mid-1900s. For instance, in the Princess' Room, there is said to be a painting that was, apparently, the preliminary sketch for Van Dyck's famous *'Children of Charles I.'* These paintings also include works by other celebrated painters such as Godfrey Kneller and Sir Joshua Reynolds.

For all its splendor and wonder, the true majesty of Raynham Hall lies in its history and the legend that surrounds it - the story of the Brown Lady who haunts the hallowed halls. She is called the 'Brown Lady' in reference to the brown brocade dress she is seen wearing.

Charles Townshend was the second Viscount Townshend of Raynham Hall. He served as a leader in the House of the Lords in England and was born in the year 1674. The Brown Lady of Raynham Hall is none other than his wife, Lady Dorothy Walpole, who was the sister of Robert Walpole. Robert Walpole was a statesman who was generally accepted as being the first Prime Minister of Great Britain. While people debate about the exact dates of his term, the years between 1721 and 1742 are recognized as being under his

Ghost Stories

control, and he holds the record for being the longest-serving Prime Minister in Britain's history. He is regarded to be one of the first people to have integrated the rising power of the House of Commons and the diminishing strength of the House of Lords, thus attempting to establish more equality.

Robert Walpole may have been quite the gentleman, but his brother-in-law, Viscount Charles Townshend, was not. Charles was notorious for his short temper. In the meantime, Lady Dorothy, who was rumored to be the prettiest of the Walpole sisters, caught the wandering eye of Charles Townshend, who was then already married to Lady Elizabeth Pelham. He asked for her hand in marriage, and it was not long before Lady Dorothy was sent to Raynham Hall, which she would continue to haunt after her life on this earth had ended.

Accounts tell us that there was a political rivalry between Walpole and Townshend, even though the two of them were neighbors in Norfolk. Their personal dissension hit terminal velocity when Walpole decided to build Houghton Hall in Norfolk as well. Townshend believed that Raynham was the

35

crowning glory of Norfolk and that any other mansion would only diminish and degrade its grandeur. He was not ready to admit the loss of power and control that came with another politician, one as strong as Walpole, establishing a base near his own.

So was Lady Dorothy a peace offering from Walpole's side? Was she a gift to please Townshend into accepting reality and burying the hatchet? We will never know if Walpole knew that he caused his sister to be collateral damage in his personal fight with Townshend. Neither will we know if the Lady herself was interested in, or even accepted this marriage. Her motivations and aspirations are lost to the pages of history.

What has been speculated, however, is that she was having an affair with Lord Wharton at the time of her wedding, and perhaps even before her marriage. Lord Thomas Wharton, the first Marques of Wharton, was a man notorious for his debauched and hedonistic lifestyle. Born in the year 1648, he was a nobleman who also served as a politician. His genuine interest, though, lay in drinking, partying, and

Ghost Stories

leading a life of pleasure and self-indulgence. He had multiple lovers and was quite the hedonist.

Some records indicate that he may have once broken into a church while drunk and then gone on to sacrilegiously relieve himself against the communion table, as well as in the pulpit of the church. Whether this is true or not we do not know as there is little hard evidence that proves it. However, when he was publicly accused of it in the House of the Lords, Wharton was speechless and could not offer a proper response, indicating that he was guilty of the crime in question.

What is truly sad is that, despite all his debauchery, he was a man of great wit, charm, and intelligence. In fact, he was one of the strongest politicians in Aylesbury, and his voice was instrumental in the *Ashby vs. White* case, which is famous in the UK for having established the right to vote and equality for all.

It is little wonder then that Lady Dorothy, attracted to his wit, charm, and power, allegedly consented to be his lover before her marriage was fixed to Charles Townshend, and this carried on even after the wedding. It was Townshend's discovery of her illicit affair that led to her death.

It was not the kind of crime of the mad, murderous rage of a jealous husband who grabs the nearest weapon he could find. It was, instead, a much crueler, painful death that Lady Dorothy went through. Charles Townshend abandoned her and left her locked up in the family home all by herself. She was left to die alone and discarded within the walls of Raynham Hall. Her husband did not even allow her to visit with her children. Can you imagine that? Being trapped in a mansion that serves as your prison, with no one to interact with, thrown there by your husband and abandoned by your lover? Lord Wharton certainly did not try to free her or help her in any way. Slowly, Lady Dorothy probably went mad.

At that time, there was an outbreak of smallpox. When poor Lady Dorothy caught the disease, no one was there to nurse her back to health. Alone, desolate, and sick, Lady Dorothy she may have gotten so weak in body and spirit that she lost all her will to live. You could say that Dorothy was already haunting Raynham Hall even before she died. Finally, in

Ghost Stories

1726, her sickness and her soul made her so weak, she eventually passed away and was buried on the grounds.

Another theory proposed is that Lord Wharton's wife, the famous writer, poet and aristocrat Lady Mary Wortley Montagu, may have been the cause of Lady Dorothy's grief. The Countess of Wharton was allegedly in a rage over her husband's affair with Dorothy that she deceived her by inviting her to her home. She conspired with Charles Townshend, and it was at her cunning direction that Lady Dorothy was to be fatally trapped inside Raynham Hall.

Whatever the real reasons were that led Lady Dorothy to this fatal end, what is sure is that it was a slow and cruel demise. No wonder the anger within her soul ensured that she would not rest. Her spirit, still looking for vengeance or even justice, still wanders the grounds, waiting for release.

Charles Townshend himself died in 1738. He spent his last years at Raynham, possibly being haunted by the appearance of his wife's ghost. However, that was not enough for her restless spirit to move on. She was still angry, sad and filled with pain.

The first recorded sighting of the Brown Lady happened in 1835. Colonel Loftus went to Raynham Hall to spend Christmas there. He was walking into his room late in the night when he caught sight of a figure in front of his room.

It was a woman, dressed in a brown brocade gown. When he tried to get a better look at her face, she vanished. The next evening, she appeared to him again, and this time, Loftus made a note of her empty eye sockets and her glowing countenance. When news of this haunting came out, it was not a surprise that members of the house staff resigned from their jobs and decided to leave the cold manor permanently.

More people started to tell personal stories of their own encounter with the ghost. Whether this Brown Lady was Lady Dorothy was something that people did not think about at that time. She was only called the Brown Lady who appeared and terrorized unsuspecting victims. The second reported sighting is a second-hand account. Captain Frederick Marryat, a writer and a sailor, and who was a friend of author Charles Dickens, was apparently the next person to have seen her. While he did not comment on his

Ghost Stories

experience, his son, Florence Marryat, gave a detailed account of his father's brush with the paranormal.

By this time, the locals had seen the Brown Lady often enough that Raynham Hall was getting a reputation as a haunted mansion. Marryat wanted to find out the truth. He asked to spend a night in the room that was supposedly haunted. He believed that the 'haunting' was merely local smugglers using Raynham Hall as their home base, and who wanted to keep people away from their goods.

Florence Marryat said that his father stayed in the room that had the portrait of the apparition. It was by comparing the ghost to this portrait that people realized it was Lady Dorothy who was haunting them. It was in this room that she was most often seen and was possibly the room in which she took her last breath. Marryat slept in that room each night with a revolver stashed beneath his pillow. For the first two days, there were no signs of anything paranormal. On the third night, though, two young men called on him for help in authenticating a gun that was arriving from London that day. As he left the room, he took his revolver, joking that it was for safety, "in case we meet the Brown Lady..."

41

Dressed in nothing but a shirt and trousers (an indecent sort of attire for that era), Marryat accompanied the men down the hall. Initially, they caught a glimpse of a lamp that was coming towards them. The two young men with him figured that it was probably one of the mansion's ladies on her way to visit the nursery. The men moved quietly so that they would not appear in front of the woman, mainly because Marryat was dressed in what was considered to be immodest clothing and did not want to offend a noble lady.

As they watched from their vantage point, Marryat was stunned to realize that she was wearing the infamous brown brocade gown, and she was none other than the Brown Lady. Pulling out his revolver, he was about to pull the trigger and demand the truth when she stopped at the door behind which he was hiding. Marryat claimed that she lifted the lamp she was carrying to highlight her sunken features and then grinned at him in a "malicious and diabolical manner."

An ordinary man might have frozen in such a situation. Marryat, on the other hand, yanked his revolver hard and discharged the bullet right into her face. It passed right through her and lodged itself in the wall behind her, as the

Ghost Stories

Brown Lady herself vanished into thin air. Marryat returned home and never again attempted to go back to Raynham Hall to seek out the Brown Lady.

The next reported sighting of Lady Dorothy happened in 1926, which the then Lady Townshend recorded. Her son and his friend had been playing on the staircase together when they felt an unusual chill and caught sight of the ghost. It wasn't long before they realized that she was the same woman in the portrait, and they drew the conclusion that it was the Brown Lady, Lady Dorothy, who had been trapped within the manor and died inside its walls.

The most infamous sighting of the Brown Lady happened in the year 1936 when she was captured on film and nationalized in *Country Life* magazine, catapulting her and Raynham Hall to fame. On the 19th of September 1936, Captain Hubert Provand, a photographer based in London, came to Raynham Hall with his assistant, Indre Shira. They both worked for *Country Life* magazine and wanted to take pictures of the manor for an article. It goes without saying that they were also intrigued by the mansion's history and

43

ghastly legend. Their photograph was one of the first ghost pictures ever captured, and this garnered so much attention.

They had just taken a picture of the Hall's main staircase when Shira caught sight of the veiled form floating down the stairs. Shira pressed down on the trigger and captured the picture, but it was not until they developed the picture that they realized that they had caught the Brown Lady on camera. They got the photograph along with their entire story published in *Country Life* magazine making them famous almost overnight.

Noted paranormal investigator, Harry Price, came to interview them. He claimed that their story was legitimate, given that they did not even realize they were capturing a ghost on camera. The negative was verified as not having been tampered with so it can be assumed that it is authentic. Logic dictates that when all other possibilities are eliminated, the truth is what's left, no matter how bizarre or unbelievable it is. And the fact is that the Brown Lady exists and two amateur photographers captured her on film.

Over the years, various people have studied the photograph and argued the truth behind it. Modern science has

Ghost Stories

examined the picture time and again, and each time, results have been inconclusive. There is a claim that the image could be an accidental double exposure or that light got inside of the camera by mistake, or even that Shira and Provand faked the photograph. Even if any of these theories were true, it only proves that the *photograph* is a fake, and not that the Brown Lady herself is.

Even after the picture was published, sightings of the Brown Lady haunting that room and the staircase continued although they have dwindled down in number through the years. The late Marchioness of Townsend reported having seen her several times in the late 1960s, and many of the housekeeping staff talk about the cold drafts and lights typical of a haunting within the manor.

The truth is that she still lingers in the hallowed halls, waiting for a release from her prison. Such a tragedy, trapped by her own family and left to die, her mind going insane, all this anger and hate inside her with no closure. She still roams the manor, haunted by what happened centuries ago, waiting for the day when, once and for all, she will be able to leave Raynham Hall.

Hannah J. Tidy

Ghost Stories

Chapter 3-

Ghosts - Emails from the Other Side

Jack Froese

A modern and relatively recent story, the tale of Jack Froese was first told through the personal accounts of those affected by it. This story can be one of horror, as well as joy, depending on how you would personally cope with and view the death of someone close to you. Some may find it deeply unsettling or horrifying, while others would find solace in the experience if they happen to have lost someone dear to them. Either way, everybody will agree that the freak occurrence described by Froese's friends and family is incredibly strange, to say the least.

Jack Froese was, in the words of his loved ones, a kind, sensitive, and well-liked man living in Dunmore, in the state of Pennsylvania. Unfortunately, he passed away at the young age of thirty-two (32) in June 2011 due to heart problems, arrhythmic complications in particular. His death was very sudden and shocked those around him, leaving them all with much grief. He was survived by his mother, Patty Froese, his longtime friend Tim Hart, and his cousin Jimmy McGraw, with whom he was close to as well.

Jack's friends and family began to accept the loss and cope with it as best as they could, moving on with their lives and coming to terms with life without him. This would have been an ordinary story of human loss, grief, and letting go of someone special, had it not been for the bizarre events that began to occur a few months after Jack's death.

In November of 2011, Tim Hart and Jimmy McGraw were each stunned to receive separate emails from their deceased friend's email account. The messages were rather personal in nature and referred to some of the final conversations and situations that they found themselves in with Jack not long before his untimely death. These unique details infused the

Ghost Stories

emails with a striking level of credibility and authenticity, which made it very difficult for his friends to brush them off as a big prank by someone who had hacked into Jack's account.

Both Tim Hart and Jimmy McGraw also believe, as they have stated in an interview given to the BBC, that nobody could have possibly known the password for Jack's email account and that a case of cyber hacking was very unlikely. Both Hart and McGraw discussed and showed the contents of the emails they received from the deceased in the BBC's TV interview.

The message that Hart received stood out in his email inbox, not only because of the deceased sender, but also due to its eerie subject title, which concisely stated, "I'm watching." When Tim Hart first saw this message, he remembered that he turned as white as a sheet with utter disbelief. After the initial shock had faded and after he got a grip on himself and his emotions, he opened the email and was greeted by the familiar, light-hearted tone of voice in the email message, characteristic of the Jack Froese he knew and loved. This message from "Jack" read, "Did you hear me? I'm at your house. Clean your f***ing attic!"

This was especially shocking to Tim since it wasn't long before his friend's death that Jack commented jokingly on how Tim's attic was in desperate need of cleaning up. They shared this verbal exchange in a private setting, and Hart maintains that nobody else knew about it and would possibly even think of saying such a thing in an email message. Needless to say, he was unsure what to make of the email in the end, but he still replied to the received message, hoping to elicit some kind of response from beyond the grave. Unfortunately, no response that we know of ever came about.

Similarly, the email sent to Jimmy McGraw pertained to his personal matters as well, but this time, regarding issues that occurred after Jack's death on June of 2011. McGraw explains in the interview that he broke his ankle about a week before the received email in November 2011, on his way to work. In the message McGraw received, "Jack" asked how he was doing and told him that he knew he was going to sustain his injury, and that he tried to warn him. "Jack" then

Ghost Stories

told him that he ought to be careful, made a couple of very short personal remarks, and ended with his name as a signature. McGraw said that during the time when he was recovering, following his ankle injury and accident, he saw very few people, which only included a couple of friends and a few family members.

Despite the initial bewilderment brought about by the eerily personal emails from their departed friend, the people Jack left behind soon came to terms with what had happened. Of course, it remains unclear whether this bizarre correspondence was a very distasteful and cruel prank, or actual documented communication with the deceased Jack Froese from the realm beyond our own. Many people would probably be very disturbed if they received any sort of message or a perceived sign from their dead loved ones, but this wasn't the case with the folks that Jack left behind in Dunmore, Penn.

Jack Froese's mother Patty told the interviewers that the emails delighted some people while they disturbed others. For her personally, she accepted them with an open heart and told Jack's loved ones that the messages were a gift from him and that they should accept them as such. She didn't give much thought to whether or not they were just a cruel prank. Instead, she was grateful for the mere fact that these mysterious emails got people to keep talking again about her son and kept his memory alive.

Hart and McGraw were of a very similar mind on the subject as well. Hart said that he didn't really care whether he was being pranked or not, and that he wholeheartedly accepted the advice from Jack's mother. He said that he would take this mystery however he wanted to, but accepting it as a good thing in the end. McGraw had very similar feelings, and he described how hard he was hit by his cousin's sudden departure, explaining that he viewed the emails as Jack's attempts to help him feel better and move on from his death. He concluded that he liked the fact that he received the mysterious and unexplained email in the first place.

Dealing with death and loss is such a personal and subjective experience that we each must go through in our own way. This story has that effect on the audience since it can vary and be very subjective, depending on the person hearing it for the first time. It's possible that these emails were sent by

Ghost Stories

someone close to the recipients who thought of a very distasteful way to pull a nasty trick on his or her friends. But then again, we don't know if they were also somehow sent by Jack Froese from beyond the grave in an effort to tease his dear loved ones for one last time, in the way that they knew he liked to do. Either way, Jack's inner circle got something good out of the whole experience and found a sort of closure in the mysterious messages, helping them to eventually move on. How would you have felt receiving such an unexplained and eerie correspondence from the realm of the unknown?

Hannah J. Tidy

Chapter 4 -

Ghosts- To Raise the Devil

The Ghosts of Taunton State Hospital

Many ghost stories are about sightings of single apparitions of spirits whose common tales begin with some gruesome or traumatic experience resulting in a very tragic end. These souls sometimes get trapped in the locale where such vile crimes were committed. But when a place is subject to the constant visitation of more than a single spirit, then that story would be, truly, a horrifying haunting.

Asylums have always been sites of hauntings and for good reason. During earlier times, these places were treated as the graveyard for the mentally ill. During the pre-dawn of modern medicine and enlightened interpretations to psychology, the insane and the mentally disturbed were discarded by their families and sent to faraway institutions. The doctors at these institutions had a freehand with performing horrific experiments on these patients, all in the dubious name of science. Little wonder, then, that the ghosts of the hundreds of disturbed innocents, who were tortured and killed, haunt many of these old asylums.

Of these many asylums, the Taunton State Hospital, located in Massachusetts, was one of the most horrific places where the Devil himself was said to have walked through the halls. Opened in 1854, it was formerly called the State Lunatic Hospital in Taunton and served as the second state asylum. What is ironic is that it was built per the specifications of a doctor named Thomas Kirkbride, who advocated that all mentally ill patients must be treated with care and compassion. They could be best treated through positivity and good feelings, not by ostracizing them or fearing them as most people were inclined to do.

The building of the hospital followed his designs, including a large campus for patients to wander around, with recreational rooms and comfortable bedrooms. The patients

Ghost Stories

were supposed to be given sunlight, fresh air, good food and a good space to move around in. It had bridgeways to keep the wards connected to the hospital's infirmary wing. The hospital was aesthetically beautiful and quite pleasing to the eye.

The outer beauty, however, could not hide the inner ugliness that was taking place in its hallowed halls. Its history is bloody, murderous and painful. Thousands of patients were tortured here and a number of staff members, over the years, have reported stories of being victims themselves of some paranormal phenomenon.

Taunton itself hosted a number of infamous people within its walls. Thomas Hubbard Sumner, the inventor of the Sumner Line, was one such patient who spent his last days in this hospital. Convicted serial killer Jane Toppan was also sentenced to life here, and her story is quite a chilling tale. Toppan, who lost her mother when she was just a child, was raised by her father who was an alcoholic and eccentric madman nicknamed 'Kelley the Crack.' He left his two daughters at the Boston Female Asylum and vanished. Jane was then adopted as the servant of the well-to-do Toppan family, whose last name she took.

As she grew up and trained to be a nurse, she started using her patients as her guinea pigs, dosing them with various drugs such as morphine and atropine. She claimed that the sight of her patients when they were close to death, aroused her sexually. She would dose them, get into bed with them and hold them close as they passed away. She later moved back to her hometown where she killed her foster sister, as well as attempted to seduce her widowed brother-in-law after the gruesome fact. With her foster sister dead, she tried to convince her sister's husband that she loved him by poisoning him, only to nurse him back to health. She also poisoned herself to gain sympathy from him. These attempts to get the attention of her brother-in-law did not work, and he sent her away from their home. Investigations of her previous murders led to her arrest where she confessed to having killed more than 30 people. She was sentenced to life at the Taunton State Asylum. Her ghost, no doubt, still haunts the halls, drawing people closer to death and holding them tight as they pass into the void.

Ghost Stories

Madness, violence, and murder ran rampant within the halls of Taunton. While many patients housed within the facility were genuinely disturbed, what was far more frightening were the secret activities of the doctors and staff members themselves at Taunton.

According to local legend, Taunton was the site of cult activity and devil worship. It was said that patients were routinely sacrificed to Satan and other demons. It was stated that staff members allegedly brought the most helpless of patients down to the basement to be offered to the Dark Lord as sacrificial lambs. Some patients, who, after having heard the rumors of what had transpired below the hospital, refused to be brought down to the basement. Because of this, they lost their outdoor privileges.

What exactly happened in the basement? We can only speculate. A huge number of staff members report that the basement remains icy cold even in the middle of summer, and there are numerous cold spots that move throughout the entire hospital. Even today, strange markings in blood cover the walls of the basement where these rumored murder rituals took place. No doubt, possibly hundreds of lost souls are still trapped within these haunted corridors, trying to reach out in the only way they know how.

One staff member once decided that he would like to see the truth for himself. As he walked down the length of the stairs, he stopped on the final step, unable to move further. Rooted to the spot, he described what could only be a paranormal experience. As he closed his eyes, he felt every single case of torture and pain that each of the tormented souls trapped within the hospital was put through. He raced back upstairs and resigned from his job that very day. Even now, he has trouble explaining what he saw and went through and remains traumatized by his experience.

It isn't just the hospital that is haunted. The woods that surround it are likewise as ghastly terrifying, as satanic rituals were allegedly conducted there as well. Groaning moans, desperate cries, and anguished calls for help can still be heard at night. Banging noises are a daily occurrence, as are flashing lights and strange, cold drafts.

Some of the later staff reported seeing a man in white walking around the corridors of the third floor. He flickers in and out of visibility, becoming physical and then

Ghost Stories

vanishing, coming and going as he wishes. Sometimes, he is simply a shadow that crawls across the wall in a slow, terrifying manner, as though looking for something. Other times, he becomes a solid figure, striding across the hallway in a rage. The figure is always a male, but no one has ever seen his full face. Residents have reported that he stands in the corner of their rooms and watches them silently. Switch on the lights, and he vanishes, his face always hidden in the shadows.

Could he be one of the many victims who was tortured and killed at Taunton? Or is he the Devil himself, waiting to ensnare unsuspecting victims? Did the doctors, through their heinous acts of brutality and murder, actually manage to raise Satan himself? Is the victim or perpetrator? Or perhaps even both? We can only speculate.

The cemetery is also quite a haunting site. One resident reports a chilling story. A patient managed to escape the halls of Taunton. He ran out of the facility but tired quickly and unable to run any further, he decided to wait the night out in the graveyard. It seemed to be a good idea because no one would think to look for him within the grounds of the hospital itself.

As he crouched near a tombstone, he felt the cold, icy grip of a hand holding his shoulder tight enough to bruise it. Thinking that he had been captured, he threw his arms up, turning around to face his captor, only to see that there was utterly *nothing and no one* behind him. A second later, a soft whisper murmured into his ear, "Leave." It repeated itself again and again and again. Terrified, and out of his mind with panic, the man ran back into the hospital where he spent the rest of his days.

Were both the ghostly hand and the ghastly voice that of a ghost attempting to warn him to escape the halls of Taunton? Or was it the Devil himself, trying to frighten the man into staying? One can only wonder.

Doors slam, lights flash, and icy chills occur within the rooms of Taunton at any given time. The shadows dance, but not in a happy manner. The silhouettes speak of horror unimaginable, of the hundreds of innocents whose blood was shed in an attempt to bring the Devil to life within the walls of Taunton. It is not surprising that this has become one of the most haunted places in the United States of America.

Taunton State Hospital, supposedly a sanctuary for the mentally disturbed where they might find peace of mind and solace of spirit, had become otherwise. The doctors, meant to be their caretakers, turned into their captors as they used them as sacrificial lambs for slaughter, cutting into them and offering them up as bait for their satanic rituals.

Whether it was psychotic criminals like Jane Toppan or the innocent victims whose families shipped them off to Taunton because they could not be bothered with caring for an insane individual, thousands of people were trapped within the halls of Taunton State Hospital, their lives ending in terrifying tragedy. Even today, their souls have not found a way out of the madhouse and remain inside this prison, long after their bodies have died and become rotten under the ground.

Hannah J. Tidy

Chapter 5 –

Paranormal - When Science Collides with the Paranormal

The Possession of Julia

There is seldom a case of possession, haunting, ghost sighting, or anything else relating to the paranormal that people from the fields of science take notice of. And if they do care to comment on the stories and give their opinions, they are almost exclusively highly skeptical and even ridicule the idea. After all, if anybody were to debunk a particular paranormal story, it would usually be the men and women of science. It is their life's calling to seek material evidence that can be put to the test, proving any theory beyond any doubt and basing their understanding of reality on that which can be observed clearly in nature through our five senses.

Hannah J. Tidy

Once in a while, however, a fascinating case of the paranormal crops up, which the scientific community takes into account and is seriously investigated and carefully documented. Such is the story of Dr. Richard Gallagher, who is a board-certified psychiatrist and a professor of clinical psychiatry at the New York Medical College. In the year 2008, Dr. Gallagher spoke of a particular case regarding a woman referred to simply as "Julia," although her real identity remains confidential. He brought forth the case through an article he published in the New Oxford Review. He called what was happening to Julia a "contemporary, clear-cut case of demonic possession." Furthermore, the doctor, himself apparently a believer in the phenomenon, said that this case would prove very convincing to even the firmest of skeptics.

What appeared to be just another instance of a highly disturbed, tormented soul, at first, soon started to seem like much, much more than that. According to the doctor's testimony, as well as those of quite a few other people involved, the affliction that struck Julia's mind and soul may not have been of this dimension. The witnesses to some of her demonic episodes included priests, assistants, deacons,

Ghost Stories

nuns, and psychiatrists. Believe it or not, all of these people were present to see the extraordinary paranormal occurrences in some of Julia's worst episodes, including levitation.

Everything points to Julia consulting with priests and Dr. Gallagher of her own volition. Wishing to undergo a Roman Catholic exorcism, Julia sought the assistance from a priest. Simultaneously, Gallagher, in his capacity as a psychiatric professional, was called in to rule out the possibility of mental illness. The doctor had no idea of what was to come.

According to what little information Gallagher disclosed about her, Julia was in her middle age, employed, and white American. Most importantly, she was very intelligent, showed no signs of mental illness, and was always reasonable and logical in her normal state. She had been a Catholic for a time, but she subsequently decided to go down a different path.

The woman had a dark, lengthy history of involvement with Satanist groups, with whom she had participated with in many satanic rituals. Over time, she began to feel that a demon, or even Satan himself, might have possessed her as her life was deteriorating rapidly on all fronts. She was certain of this by the time Gallagher and the rest of the team got involved.

In Gallagher's own words, the exorcising of Julia's supposed demons commenced with a ritual in June, on an expectedly warm day. The doctor further explained that despite the rising temperatures outside, the room where the exorcism was about to be carried out was unnaturally cold. However, the room grew warm beyond comfort as the exorcism was well underway. The intensity of the exorcism was reported to give off immense heat, which almost got to the point of forcing everybody out.

At the beginning of the exorcism, things were fairly quiet, as Julia appeared to drift away into a state of serene trance. Gallagher explained that Julia would often go into all kinds of trances repeatedly. Although dislodgment from reality is common among many mentally ill individuals, Julia's episodes were particularly marked by strange aspects. Her voice would change rapidly and oscillate between high and low pitches, sometimes sounding rather deep and intimidating. The voices seemed very unnatural and foreign

Ghost Stories

to the Julia they knew when she wasn't experiencing these states. The alleged demons would hurl insults and threats through her, and Julia referred to herself in third person. It seemed evident that the voices appeared to come from a source clearly separate from Julia's person. The voices would say that Julia belongs to them, and they would warn the team to leave her alone and give up, or they would regret it. In between the insults and the taunts, all those present observed that she made bizarre screeches, roars, and monstrous growls unbecoming of any human being. As expected, Julia had absolutely no recollection of what she was saying and doing after she would snap back to reality.

Certainly, one could have easily suggested that this was somewhat like a multiple personality disorder, a life-crippling mental illness that plagues quite a few people. However, Dr. Gallagher, being a seasoned psychiatrist, would have been the first to make such a diagnosis. Alas, this was ruled out. This became even more evident as her verbal expressions soon took quite a dizzying turn for the paranormal.

The inhuman fits of rage and the overall viciousness of these demonic outbursts were the least of what was creepy. Julia would randomly start speaking in languages such as Spanish and Latin – languages that Julia didn't speak a word of, otherwise. Furthermore, it was during these freakish episodes that Julia, or whatever entity had taken hold of her, exhibited psychic abilities as well! She made comments regarding the personal information and details of the lives of those present, although she had no way whatsoever of knowing these things. Doctor Gallagher mentioned a few specific instances of this phenomenon.

She appeared to have insight into the family life of members of the team, including deaths, tragedies, illness, and other deeply personal matters. One of the team members was shocked to hear Julia describing not only the life and personal disposition of a relative, but also the way in which he died. Julia correctly "guessed" that the relative had died of cancer and, more impressively, she also was able to say what type of cancer it was.

Similarly, she was aware that another team member's household cats had a bloody, ferocious fight among

Ghost Stories

themselves the night before. Of course, she had never seen the team member's house nor the cats. As a matter of fact, she had no early way of knowing that this person even had cats. Yet, she teased the team member with comments on how brutal the cats were to each other. When he returned to his home in a completely different city the next day, the aforementioned incident was confirmed. He didn't know his cats to ever fight like that prior to this.

You'd be wrong to think that Dr. Gallagher's account stops here. Many of Julia's attacks and demonic outbursts were very physical in nature, not just verbal and psychological. Namely, the doctor describes that she had near superhuman strength, very unbecoming of an average-size, female human being. Keeping her restrained was an incredibly difficult task, and several people were hardly enough to keep her down. Things rose to a whole new level of bizarre with the doctor's description of the horror that came next. He said that everyone in the team were terrified to see Julia begin to levitate less than a foot above the floor! In defiance of the most fundamental laws of nature, she remained in this mind-boggling state for around half an hour.

Gallagher also described Julia, or the force within her, as having telekinetic abilities. The objects in the room would fly out of place and get tossed around apparently completely on their own. Books and other things were launched from their shelves rendering the situation quite dangerous for the team in the room.

As the story goes on, Julia was apparently cleansed in the end, and the team concluded that the exorcism had most likely been successful, though Gallagher had his reservations. We'll probably never know if the alleged demon was really banished from the woman or if it had just decided to change its strategy and lie dormant as a ruse to fool the exorcists. While it could be safe to assume that the rite was successful, from the many similar stories in pop culture that we are familiar with, it is quite possible that in the future, the demon could easily be triggered into activity by any stimulus that is religious in nature. Dr. Gallagher has released very few personal details about his subject, and we don't know if he kept in touch with her after the fact. Thus, Julia's subsequent fate and course remains a mystery.

Ghost Stories

Needless to say, this particular account of demonic possession is incredibly straightforward and concrete. It shocks both logic and reason. Movies and books have tapped into these factual stories as subject matter, thus further lending them a fantastical appreciation. Stories like these are easy fodder for the skeptics when the source of the claims are suspect. Certain people are deemed unstable, prone to fantasies, and have very little credibility. Dr. Gallagher is no such individual. When a man of such standing and top qualifications writes a paper outlining this kind of finding, in such a direct and clear way, it gives the story a whole new level of unsettling reality.

Of course, that isn't to say that he is infallible and incapable of lying and making up a hoax, but there would be a lot at stake for such a man if he were to take that road. His credentials and track record in psychiatry are available for all to research and take note of. Being involved in a fabrication of a paranormal phenomenon would certainly damage his reputation and possibly hinder the career that must have taken years upon years to build. All in all, the source of information is always one of the main factors skeptics consider when looking at a story of the paranormal,

Hannah J. Tidy

using it to determine the potential validity of the information – and it should be no different in this instance as well.

Chapter -6

Ghosts - Erzsébet Báthor

The Real Queen Ravenna

You probably remember hearing the story of Snow White for the first time when you were a small child. Most likely, if you grew up in the United States, the Disney version of the story is the one that stands out in your mind. In it, Snow White becomes the subject of envy by a jealous Queen who wishes to be the most beautiful woman in the kingdom. But as the Queen's magic mirror informs her, this is not the case, as Snow White is the most beautiful in the land. The Queen promptly decides to have her slaughtered immediately. The Huntsman that is supposed to kill poor Snow White takes pity on her instead and lets her escape unharmed. Snow White then meets seven dwarves who help her on her journey, and in the end, she is sweetly united with her Prince

Charming. A typically happy ending for a rosy Disney story made for the movies.

However, the modern movie *"Snow White and the Huntsman"* (2012) may be closer to the true origins of the fairy tale. The Queen, depicted here as Queen Ravenna, is obsessed with youth and beauty, to the point where she bathes in young girl's virgin blood to retain her astonishing beauty. This might sound extremely far-fetched and too gruesome to be true, but I assure you, the Blood Queen existed in real life.

When the Brothers Grimm first wrote down the story of Snow White back in 1812 in their first collection of "Grimm's Fairy Tales," the story of a real Blood Queen was already deeply ingrained in the local legends of Upper Hungary (now known as modern-day Slovakia). A diabolical and noble-born woman named Countess Erzsébet Báthory de Ecsed (1560-1614), had walked the earth for 54 short years, and during that time, was the evil mastermind of such a horrendous amount of bloodshed that she still holds the Guinness World Record as the most prolific female serial killer, with an estimated number of over 650 murders to her name.

I know what you are thinking, dear Readers. "But wait, this is a real woman, what does this story have to do with ghosts?" Just be patient, dear Readers, and wait and see! Let's start with the gory story from the very beginning, and you will find out how ghostly and otherworldly this bloody piece of history truly is.

Erzsébet, or Elizabeth, was born in the town of Nyírbátor in Eastern Hungary. She was part of the local aristocracy as she was the niece of the Hungarian nobleman Stephen Báthory, King of the Polish-Lithuanian Commonwealth and the Prince of Transylvania. As a privileged member of nobility, Elizabeth grew up to be quite the spoiled child, always given whatever she wanted and everything that her heart could desire. Perhaps it was because of this background growing up that made Elizabeth feel that she deserved anything that she could ever want, no matter what the cost or effect was. The lines between good and evil blurred with all the indulgences afforded her from such a young age. It certainly can't be said that her future odd behavior grew out of misfortune in her early childhood development.

Elizabeth was engaged at the tender age of 11 years old and married her fiancé Ferenc Nádasdy when she turned 15. Because she had a more prominent social standing than her new husband, she did not change her name and remained Elizabeth Báthory. Ferenc Nádasdy would go on to become the leader of the Hungarian army and spent most of his time away on battles, and eventually, he would become a war hero. This left Elizabeth home alone at their shared household in Sárvár, Csejte Castle, in the Little Carpathians near Trencsén (now Trenčin), for very long periods of time, completely left to her own devices. On the surface, Elizabeth Báthory appeared to be the devoted wife of a war hero, a mother to numerous children, a dutiful manager of Nádasdy's business affairs and estates, and also a social benefactor to the nearby townspeople.

But people in the kingdom soon began to suspect horrendous evil-doings happening in Csejte Castle as more and more young female servants, who were lured to Báthory castle with promises of well-paid work as maidservants,

Ghost Stories

seemed to vanish into thin air. Between the years of 1602 and 1604, when hushed rumors and talk of the demonic atrocities being committed against innocent young women of Elizabeth Báthory's household spread like wildfire in the kingdom, a courageous Lutheran minister by the name of István Magyari filed formal complaints against her publicly and also at the authorized court in Vienna. Finally, around 1610, King Matthias II assigned György Thurzó, the Palatine of Hungary (or the highest-ranking official in the Kingdom of Hungary), to lead an investigation of the alleged bloody affairs of Elizabeth at Csejte Castle in Sárvár.

The ongoing investigation and collection of evidence against Elizabeth Báthory between 1610 and 1611 yielded testimonies from over 300 witnesses. It was discovered that, although Báthory had started by only killing peasant girls who were adolescent daughters of the local peasants, her murderous reach had greedily broadened to include the youthful virgins and daughters of the lesser gentry who were sent to Elizabeth's female quarters at the castle in Sárvár to learn court etiquette. As the investigators, lead by György Thurzó himself, arrived at Csejte Castle in Sárvár on December 30, 1610, they were horrified to find the Countess

Elizabeth in the very act of torturing numerous young girls, with others still locked up in the castle, awaiting their turn for torture and an eventual gruesome death at the hands of the Blood Queen.

As Elizabeth Báthory was finally brought to justice, the true gruesomeness of all her illicit actions became apparent. Hundreds of witnesses stepped forward to indict her. Not only had these demonic acts occurred within Csejte Castle in Sárvár, but also in the Countess' properties in Németkeresztúr, Pozsony (today known as Bratislava), and even Vienna. She had abducted, captured, tortured, bled, and had even eaten body parts of hundreds of innocent young women. Some of the torturous, blood extracting methods included sticking her victims with pins and needles, and even smearing them with honey to be attacked by swarms of bees and ants. One girl even attested that Elizabeth cut off parts of her body, boiled them, and forced her to eat her own flesh.

But what exactly was the true and demented motivation of the Countess for the heinous acts that she had committed over the years before she was caught? The most popular theory at the time was that she sought immortality and never-fading beauty. Blood is life, after all, and through it's continuous flow and consumption, the Blood Queen chose to ingest gallons of this fresh life-force from innocent victims into her own body. Some even say that she regularly bathed in gallons of warm blood, freshly procured by her ghoulish accomplices who would kill the victims and siphon the blood in the bathing chambers of the Countess, for the preservation of her youthful looks and beautiful skin. No price was too large for Countess Elizabeth Báthory to pay to obtain the keys to immortality. Bathing in the blood of young virgins would keep her young and give her eternal life. Her appetite had become insatiable. An extreme blood lust had taken over her world until the day that she died while she was imprisoned in solitary confinement in Csejte Castle on August 21, 1614.

But the question is, did the Blood Queen succeed? Does she still live on, but perhaps now as only as a malevolent ghost? If you ask some scholars, they will tell you that she died in solitary confinement in her cursed castle. But there are mysterious circumstances surrounding her death that leave the door open to other options. A guard was the one who supposedly found Elizabeth dead in her room, while she was under house arrest after her trial. She was buried in the church of Csejte, but because there was a public uproar over her body being laid to rest in holy ground there after all she had done, it was exhumed to be buried again in her birth home of Ecsed where it was supposedly laid to rest in the Báthory Family Crypt. But in the present time, the location of her body is largely unknown. Many speculate that she still walks the world today, even if only as a ghost. Perhaps she is simply waiting for the opportune time to strike again. Our blood runs cold thinking of who her next victim might be?

Chapter -7

Ghosts - The Winchester House

The Never-Ending Construction

If you grew up in the United States, the name Winchester is probably as familiar to you as Ford, Colt, and the Wright brothers. Yes, the Winchester family we are talking about started with the main man, William Wirt Winchester, who developed the modernized "Henry Rifle" that was a favorite of American soldiers during the Civil War. The "Winchester Repeating Arms Company" popularized and invented several forms of the modern firearm and the family made their considerable fortune because of weapons contracts with the government as well as private sales made at the time. In fact, this company that was founded by William

Winchester back in 1857 is the same company that is still in existence today.

This is all on public record, but there is another closely-related story that is not quite as cut and dry as these hard facts. Did you also know that the Winchesters are connected with one of the most famous ghost stories in the history of the United States? This factual story will have the hairs on the back of your neck stand straight up!

It all began at the height of the Civil War with the elaborate wedding of William Wirt Winchester and Sarah Pardee in New Haven, Connecticut on September 30, 1862. William was the heir to the Winchester empire that his father, Oliver Winchester, had built. Sarah was a popular and loved woman in the community because of her talented musical skills, fluency in several foreign languages and her innate charm. At the time of William and Sarah's marriage, it seemed like the world was their oyster. It wasn't long, however, before things changed drastically and sadly, for the worse.

Four years after their wedding, on July 15, 1866, Sarah gave birth to their first daughter, Annie Pardee Winchester. But

Ghost Stories

that was when the first misfortune struck Sarah as her baby died after only a few days of life when she contracted a debilitating illness known as "marasmus" where the body of the child literally wastes away until eventual death. The baby passed away on July 24 and this nearly pushed Sarah towards the edge of madness with her grief. Sarah was utterly distraught for some time after, but at least she had her husband William by her side to comfort her. The death of the baby was so impacting, though, that the couple never had another child.

A year shy of their 20th wedding anniversary, misfortune struck once again, and Sarah's husband William succumbed to pulmonary tuberculosis and died on March 7, 1881. Sarah became a multi-millionaire overnight, receiving an incredible inheritance of over $20 million dollars, as well as 48.9 percent of William's family business, the Winchester Repeating Arms Company, with an income of around $1000 dollars a day. But all of Sarah's newly received wealth and family fortune could not help ease the pain and suffering that she was going through over the deaths of both her husband and only child. Her grief completely eradicated any ounce of joy from her life, and she was heartbroken.

It was in this fragile, highly-emotional state that Sarah was approached by a friend of hers to seek out a Spiritualist medium to converse with her husband, William so that she might have some closure after his untimely death. Unbeknownst to Sarah, this decision to consult with the supernatural and spirits from the other realm would eventually lead her down the path of the construction of the world-famous Winchester House. When Sarah finally met with the Spiritualist, she was told that the ghost of her husband, William Winchester, was present. The medium relayed to Sarah an important message from William. "He is telling me to let you know that there is a terrible curse on your family and this is the reason for the deaths of both himself and your child. It will soon claim your life too unless you do something to stop it. This curse is the direct result of the deaths of thousands of people from the creation of the firearms produced by the Winchester family company. The spirits of the dead now seek vengeance." Sarah was also told that she must pack up, sell her properties in New Haven, and make a trail for herself in the West, on the path of the setting sun. Sarah was also told not to worry, she would be guided on this journey by the spirit of her husband William, and when she finally set eyes on the right property for her new home in the West, her heart would recognize it. The vengeful spirits filled by the weapons of destruction by the Winchester family would keep attacking Sarah because they were not at rest and they needed a home. If Sarah were to provide it for them by building her new house in order to start her life again, she would live. But there was a caveat to this secret for Sarah's life, the spirit of William said. It was that she would have to keep building this house so that she would not come into any mortal harm. If she were to stop at any time, she would surely die. Sarah believed wholeheartedly in everything that was relayed to her by the ghost of her husband, William.

She immediately sold her dwelling in New Haven and started traveling west. Sarah continued all the way until she reached San Jose, California, where she bought a 162-acre estate with a six-bedroom home from a local doctor. With the psychic's message from the afterlife in her mind, she immediately began construction on the home, fearful of the possible consequences should she ignore the spiritualist's warnings.

Hannah J. Tidy

Upon buying the 162-acre estate as her new home, Sarah set to work on the strangest mansion ever built on the face of this Earth. She had no formal blueprints for her house construction project and for the next 36 years, she employed 22 carpenters hard at work all year round, 24 hours on the clock. The workers kept building and rebuilding, altering and demolishing, changing and constructing each and every new wing and area of the Winchester House. Through the years, the house grew to and formed into 26 rooms with no plans of halting construction. Every morning, Sarah would meet with her construction foreman to discuss her hand-sketched plans for building work to be done that day. There was always a method to Sarah's design madness and sometimes if some of her room plans were not executed to her liking, she would order the workers to just build a room around the old one.

Amidst all the chaos of the never-ending construction, Sarah became obsessed with keeping the spirits satisfied. Some people say she would even arrange dinners and set the table so that it would include her ghostly spirit guests. The spirit of her husband, however, did not visit her again. The Winchester House continued its chaotic expansion, and by

Ghost Stories

1906, it had reached an unprecedented height of seven stories tall. But despite all the stress, fear and constant re-construction building work throughout her life, Sarah Winchester lived to the ripe old age of 83 years old.

So much of what was going on in her mind will forever remain a mystery, as Sarah was a very private woman and left no written records of the second half of her life. Although the exact number is unclear, it is estimated that the home contained around 160 rooms. The home's design is akin to a maze due to its unique construction that counting the rooms is almost impossible. Today it is registered as a California Historical Landmark and is open to the public under the name of The Winchester Mystery House.

Most people who visit say that they can still feel the presence of evil spirits in the home. Workers have heard footsteps, moving furniture, and other odd occurrences in the home. Whether the ghosts of those killed by Winchester firearms still live there or not is something you will have to decide for yourself. The house maintains regular visitation hours, and there are special tours that are available, some of which may include flashlights or psychics. While the house is incredibly

Hannah J. Tidy

odd shaped, and an architect's nightmare, you will also find quite a few fantastic innovations. Even though Sarah was very isolated, she kept her mind busy. Is it possible that the spirits helped her in her building endeavors? We will never know for sure.

Ghost Stories

Chapter -8

Ghosts - The Flying Dutchman

Lost At Sea

We have talked about stories of both individual and group hauntings. Our next intriguing adventure involves the whole crew of an entire ghost ship! Chances are, you have heard about *The Flying Dutchman* from the huge Disney blockbuster series, *Pirates of the Caribbean*. The storyline in the movie melds myths of seafaring pirates wherein the legendary Davy Jones is tasked to captain the equally legendary ghost ship, The Flying Dutchman. While the history of the pirate idiom 'Davy Jones' locker' refers to sailors plunging to their deaths at the bottom of the sea, the *Flying Dutchman* actually existed.

Hannah J. Tidy

In the 17th century, a company called the Dutch East India Company was responsible for a considerable amount of trade over the oceans. It is most commonly believed that the vessel, which became known as the Flying Dutchman, initially was sailing for this company. The first written record found was penned by a man named George Barrington, in his book entitled, *An Account of a Voyage to New South Wales. Following is his account of the story:*

"The superstition of the sailors was a subject of which I had frequently heard, and even the report that agitated the person of whom I am going to speak; but I thought it too vague to deserve any particular credit or attention. In this quarter of the globe, it seems, a report is still propagated, that some years ago a Dutch man of war being lost off the Cape, every soul on board perished. Being in company with another vessel, this, her consort weathered the gale, and more fortunate, arrived soon after at the Cape. But having repaired their damages, and being on their return to Europe, just in the same latitude they were likewise overtaken with a heavy gale. During the night watch, it is reported they saw, or supposedly saw, a vessel crowding down upon them with a full press of sail, as if she intended nothing but to run them

Ghost Stories

down. One of the people in particular, positively affirmed, that it was either the ship that foundered in the former gale or her apparition. The weather very soon after clearing up, the real object, which was a thick dark cloud, entirely disappeared. Still, nothing could dispose the minds of the sailors of what they fancied they had seen; and they had no sooner got into port, then spreading the story like wildfire, the supposed phantom obtained the name of the Flying Dutchman. From the Dutch, the English seamen got hold of the story; so that very few of our East-Indiamen pass those seas, without having someone on board, who persuades himself that he also has seen the apparition (Barrington, p.116-117)."[1]

Barrington goes on to describe how the lead crewman of his vessel woke him in the middle of the night, telling him of the ghostly apparition he had seen just minutes before, in full belief that what he saw was indeed the Flying Dutchman.

It is thought that the captains of the two ships described by Barrington were Hendrik Van der Decken and Bernard

---

[1] Barrington, George. "An Account of a Voyage to New South Wales." *Sherwood, Neely & Jones, London.* 1810.

Fokke, both of whom were Captains for the Dutch East India Company. It is unclear who of these men in the story is the captain of the surviving ship, and who became the Flying Dutchman, as both of these Captains were known to have been lost at sea. We are aware of very little of Van der Decken, but we know that Fokke made many voyages from the Netherlands to Java, and at uncanny speeds.

Some surmise that Fokke had made a pact with the devil, wherein he was given the momentum he needed for his trading activities. If this were indeed true, it would be plausible that the captain would wager his own life and that of his crew and sail on even when faced with a storm as he approached the Cape of Good Hope. Hence the belief that Captain Bernard Fokke was none other than the fearless 'Flying Dutchman.'

There have been many tales spun around this ship and its journey. When the ship came upon a gale at sea, it is rumored that Fokke threw men overboard in order to placate the storm. Some say that the captain of the ship vowed that he would sail the seas forever until he rounded the Cape of Good Hope, but was tragically shipwrecked, thus drowning all hope of making it to safety. The story goes that because of his stubbornness, he and his crew would forever be cursed to sail the oceans, never once being allowed rest nor to set foot on any shore.

You might think that an entire ghost ship is impossible. I say to you, tell that to the hundreds of witnesses who had sightings of the famous Dutch vessel over the many years. Notable people who saw the Flying Dutchman first hand include King George V of England, as well as the famous novelist Nicholas Monsarrat. The legend is that those who are unfortunate to see it are doomed to befall calamity, or worse, death. Should you find yourself out to sea chasing some adventure, beware you never come within viewing distance to the Flying Dutchman.

Hannah J. Tidy

Chapter -9

The Paris Catacombs

Darkness Beneath the City of Light

When we think of Paris nowadays, the minds of the vast majority of us quickly turn to thoughts of love, culture, light, French cuisine, landmarks such as the Eiffel Tower, the Louvre, and other cultural marvels of this famed city. Certainly, this renowned metropolis has a lot to offer to visitors in terms of entertainment, culture, and history. However, as you may or may not know, there is a great deal that lies beneath the city streets as well.

The underground of Paris, aside from its subway network and old mining tunnels, has a frighteningly intricate web of ancient catacombs. The nature of these catacombs is such that they are a haunted place regardless of whether they have actual ghosts or demons stalking their long corridors. While ghostly haunting is not out of the question, there is one thing you can count on - these catacombs have a dark and disturbing history. The tunnels amount to a few hundred miles in length altogether, and are the eternal home to the remains of some six million people!

The catacombs were established in the first half of the 18th century. The thing about these halls of the dead is that for a lot - if not most - of these souls that inhabit them, the catacombs weren't their rightly intended resting place. These catacombs were built in order to transfer the exhumed remains from the city cemeteries for a number of reasons. Firstly, the graveyards were overflowing beyond their capacity. Secondly, there were numerous cave-ins in the cemeteries, making disease and other contamination a real threat. This is why the authorities decided to begin moving many of the dead into the underground in the period between late 18th and mid-19th century, disturbing their prior peace in the process. Most of the remains would be mere bones by the time they were approved for transportation, and a bigger part of the process was conducted under the veil of darkness.

Ghost Stories

Some of the skulls and bones are stacked in an impeccable, organized manner along the walls of the tunnels, giving an almost artistic quality to the corridors. Other remains, however, appear to have simply been thrown or unloaded into small rooms and hallways, which left them piled up in no particular order. It's safe to say, human bones can be found almost anywhere in these catacombs, and many are just scattered throughout the tunnels.

Needless to say, if there is a place in the world where ghosts and wandering souls are likely to lurk, it's here. The countless number of human remains and the fact that they were brought to the catacombs after having been laid to rest in their original graves are just fuel for stories and theories. Over the years, there have been scattered reports by visitors of what they believed were sightings and encounters with ghosts. Some have described an unrelenting feeling of being watched and stalked while they were underground, while others even said they felt somebody or something physically touching them at times. If there is something paranormal to be seen down there, one must take quite a few risks in order to get to the position of catching anything.

Hannah J. Tidy

The Catacombs of Paris have been open to the public since the 19th century, and they can be accessed via a designated, surface entrance. This is the staging area for organized tours, which can be booked. However, these tours are very limited both in their longevity and their area of sightseeing, as the official tours only focus on a tiny portion of this enormous system. This provides tourists and other curious cats with a basic idea of the sights, ambiance, and the isolation of these catacombs, but it all amounts to just a taste of the real thing in the end.

Those who have wanted to get better acquainted with the catacombs in the past have had to venture outside their comfort zone and slightly outside the bounds of the law too. The Paris catacombs can be accessed from many, many locations apart from the formal entrance. There are manholes and similar openings all over the city that leads into the catacombs. Using these access points and venturing beyond the designated touring areas is illegal and carries with it a fine, which is much less than what a lot of enthusiasts are willing to risk for their thrills.

Ghost Stories

Apart from the slight run in with the law, exploring the catacombs poses many real dangers and can cost those who dare embark upon such a journey way more than a small amount of money. A huge portion of the catacombs is off limits, and is thus not illuminated in any way and simply isn't refurbished, secured, and meant for any kind of exploration or tourism. The tunnels can get very confusing even if you have a map of the catacombs, and this is only made worse by the absolute, enveloping darkness that you'd run into. Another threat is the fact that some parts of the catacombs may be insecure, unstable, and prone to caving in or flooding. Without getting yourself killed outright, you can easily lose your way and get lost, which would almost certainly mean a slow and excruciating death within a few days.

Similar was the story of one man who ventured into the remote parts of the catacombs all by his lonesome, believe it or not. It is estimated that he started out on his journey sometime in the early 1990s. This was discerned from the footage retrieved from his camera, which was the only trace that was ever found of him. He brought this camera with him to document his feat, using the camera's night recording capability. This provided a way to illuminate his way as well, which was absolutely necessary in the total darkness that surrounded him.

The recording was simple, first-person point of view footage that he recorded by hand. The man seemed well-adjusted, determined, organized, and perfectly in control for the majority of the forty-minute recording that he left behind. He documented many of the corridors and the bones found in the crypts, as he proceeded deeper and deeper into the literal underbelly of Paris. The footage clearly showed markings on the walls, mostly arrows, which the explorer seemed to follow. It wasn't until a while into the footage that things took a strange turn and quickly spiraled out of hand. The daring individual began to move through the tunnels more erratically, soon falling into a state of outright panic. At first, it appeared as though he had lost his way and was terrified by the fact. However, his state and behavior soon began to resemble that of a person being chased. He would turn around to look back a few times, while the camera caught glimpses of more markings or drawings on the walls, the most interesting of which was one apparently depicting a person with outstretched limbs, painted on in white.

Ghost Stories

After a while of frantically rushing about through the crypts, the man does something incredibly strange. He simply drops his camera, and it seems to fall into a small puddle of water, while still recording, showing the man running into the darkness ahead of him. This peculiar action definitely further argues the case that he was not merely lost. Discarding his only source of light while being lost in pitch black seems illogical and outright insane. In the likelihood that he dropped the camera by accident, the question begged is why didn't he think to pick it up? Thus it is plausible that he was running from something or someone, and if so, from whom? Or what?

This particular story broke into the mainstream and was featured on television as well. There has been significant debate over whether or not the footage is genuine. However, this discussion is not about the location or the technical authenticity of the images, as the camcorder was indeed found in the catacombs. Furthermore, a group of explorers went into the tunnels, later on, to search for and record the same location seen in the footage, which they did. They recorded the same markings and images on the walls, including the strange, white figure. The controversy has,

103

instead, lingered over the question of how *real* the footage is. Some have speculated that it could have been staged, as part of an elaborate prank. A man may have simply gone in, recorded footage of him acting as though he is panicking, and dropped the camera for others to find and ponder over.

Whatever the case may be, nobody has ever come forward to claim authorship of the footage, and there have been cases of people getting lost in the catacombs during their history, never to be found again. This may indeed be yet another such tragedy, and if the footage wasn't staged, it's possible that there was much more to this man's tragic fate than just losing his way in the dark.

It might take many more years for us to find out what actually happened. And until that happens, we may just as well assume that his fate adds one more to the six million remains lost within the catacombs. On the other hand, the man may have gotten out just fine that very day, having quite a laugh when the footage was found and the public caught wind of it. The recording has since been uploaded to the internet for all to see and judge on their own, and something tells me that it will definitely not strike you as a joke.

Ghost Stories

Chapter -10

Hauntings - The Hands Resist Him

Haunted eBay Painting

Hannah J. Tidy

Hauntings can occur anywhere but are most often associated with a particular place where paranormal activity is very common. This haunting, however, is that of a painting. Yes, you heard me right. Even the artwork hanging in your home can be haunted. This haunting is also one of the most recent and well-known modern hauntings, and the story will leave chills running down your spine.

William Stoneham, the painter of this haunted canvas, is still alive and well and painting today. He was born in Boston, Massachusetts, where his real parents gave him up for adoption. The painting is that of a photograph that was taken of him when he was only five years old. The creepy artwork, titled "The Hands Resist Him," depicts a young boy and a young girl/doll holding a battery-like object with wires, standing together in front of a glass door with images of hands seemingly floating behind the glass panels. The painter himself agrees that it is entirely possible that the painting is haunted. On his website, he claims that he has always had a particular connection to the collective unconscious found in a specific place. According to Stoneham, "the hands are the 'other lives.' The glass door, that thin veil between waking and dreaming. The girl/doll is the imagined companion or guide through this realm."[2] According to Stoneham, the inspiration for the painting came from the following poem titled "Hands Resist Him" and penned in 1971 by R. Ponseti, Bill's ex-wife, just three years prior to the creation of the painting:

"He is of the seeing visions

His strokes reveal them

In a rush- of color, of madness

Of mystics

And his head is the highest center

It must confront its enemy,

The hands- resist him,

like the secret of his birth.

His presence is the sanctum heartbeat

Felt in darkness and in passion

---

[2] Stoneham, William. "The Hands Resist Him." *Stoneham Studios.* 2015. Web. 9 May 2016.

Its sound the sole gift to that silence."[3]

Whether you believe in ghosts or not, looking at the painting will give you the creeps. In the painting, The boy's eyes are almost non-existent as if he is squinting. His pale skin appears sickly or even lifeless. Next to him on his right stands a little girl doll with hollowed out eyes. Her mouth is turned into a frown, and her countenance resembles that of an evil spirit. These details alone make the painting eerie, but it doesn't stop there. Behind the two figures, inside the dark room, about a dozen hands are seen grasping at the glass panes of the door. No bodies are perceived, and it almost appears as if the hands are floating, disembodied in the air, trying to claw their way outside. This tableau of images is unsettling, to say the least.

Little did Stoneham know that what he created would become something of a legend. After he had completed his painting, it was sold to John Marley, a character actor who has come out in over a hundred movies and TV series' including several episodes of *The Twilight Zone,* but who is

---

[3] Stoneham, William. "The Hands Resist Him." *Stoneham Studios.* 2015. Web. 9 May 2016.

Ghost Stories

probably most known for his role as a film producer in the legendary film The Godfather. When he purchased the painting, becoming the subject of a real-life Twilight Zone episode was probably the furthest thing from his mind. Within the next 10 years, three people who dealt with the painting died suddenly. Henry J. Seldis, an immigrant from Germany and the art critic who gave the painting its first press mention and Charles M. Feingarten, the owner of the art gallery where the piece was initially displayed and who was also the person who commissioned the painting passed away. And finally, Marley himself died, but not until after he had sold the painting.

The painting vanished from the headlines for the next 26 years. It then resurfaced in an eBay listing. According to an article put out by the BBC[4], the owners were selling the painting due to its haunted nature. The children depicted in the painting were coming alive at night and stepping out of the painting into the real world! They had found the piece of art in possession of a picker who had located it behind an abandoned bar. Their eBay listing was reinforced by footage

---

[4] BBC. "The eBay Haunted Painting." *BBC*. July 2002. Web. 9 May 2016.

and photos from a webcam that captured these strange happenings at night. In just a few days the Internet was abuzz with rumors, and the listing had garnered over 30,000 page views. Reports from all over started coming out claiming people that viewed the painting experienced strange manifestations such as illness and fainting. Kim Smith, the owner of an art gallery in Grand Rapids, Michigan, finally purchased the painting.

Since his purchase, Kim has not reported any kind of paranormal activity associated with the picture. It is good to note, though, that it has remained mostly in storage and has only been shown, on request, by a handful of people.

But what if the spirits in the painting are merely lying dormant, waiting for the right opportunity to strike again? After all, it laid dormant for 26 years before wreaking terror on the lives of the family that just so happened to purchase it. Will the year 2026 bring new and frightening news about the painting? This much is true, whether you believe that the art is possessed or not, everybody that has had a glimpse of the artwork all agree that that is one creepy, haunting image.

Chapter -11

Hauntings – Robert the Doll

When Dolls Stop Being Toys

Just like our previous story, this one refers to a cursed, haunted object. The difference, however, is that if the legends are true, this object is much more than just that. The stories revolving around Robert often go way beyond merely attributing a strange aura to the doll, or mentioning how it made people feel uncomfortable. As a matter of fact, Robert has been accused of everything from breaking a few household items to causing car crashes and, most disturbingly, of being alive and very malicious.

The home of Robert the Doll has been Key West, in the state of Florida, where he has lived for over a hundred years, thus far. He is currently kept at the local Fort East Martello Museum since 1994. We'll go over the events that led to him finding a home there later on.

Even if you haven't heard this story, the chances are good that you have seen at least one of quite a few films that were inspired by the legend of Robert. There are at least a couple of them explicitly titled after the doll's name, but it's possible that other similar movies were, at the very least, drawing subtle inspiration from the legend. Movies such as the popular Chucky doll from "Child's Play" carry a similar theme. While Chucky had a very strikingly creepy look about him, Robert may not come across as all that scary to some at first, as his eeriness is more subtle.

However, even if he looks just like an ordinary doll at first glance, no doubt you will begin to see him for his true, unsettling appearance after a while of observing him. He's quite a large doll at around three feet in height, resembling a little boy in natural size. Overall, though, there is very little, except his basic humanoid shape, that makes Robert look like a human being. His minimalistic facial features make him look quite disfigured, and not in a cute way either.

Ghost Stories

Robert has a barely noticeable nose and two completely round, small, black eyes. His ears are quite pronounced, and his strange mouth appears to give off a subtle smirk. In his lap, he keeps his own toy, a stuffed toy representing a dog. And you guessed it; the dog looks fairly strange as well, with big, glaring eyes and a disproportionately large mouth. Robert himself is dressed in a white sailor's suit and wearing a sailor's cap, which some speculate was worn by his original, famous owner when he was a boy. The man in question was Robert Eugene Otto, who lived in a large Victorian style house that came to be known as the Artist House since Robert Eugene was a painter. Otto died in 1974, and he is the other half of this story.

The inception of the legend can be traced back to the year 1906 when the doll was first given to Otto by either his grandfather or his nanny, who originated from the Bahamas. These constitute the two different tales of how Otto first got his doll, and they vary from one source to the next.

The first story of origin states that the doll was brought home by Otto's grandfather from a trip to Germany, and given to the boy on his birthday. Since the doll has been in possession of a museum for over two decades now, they did their research and supposedly traced Robert as having been manufactured by Steiff, a German-based toy company. This corroborates the first story of Robert's origins.

However, there is a different theory as to where Robert came from, which many people subscribe to. Months before Robert Eugene Otto was born, his mother asked his father, Mr. Otto, to go to the Bahamas and bring home four servants to help around the house. She instructed him to ensure that one of them is a woman, who would serve as a babysitter for little Otto once he was born. However, Mr. Otto allegedly proved entirely untrustworthy during his trip, and he got the soon-to-be nanny pregnant. Needless to say, this infuriated Mrs. Otto, and she cruelly punished the native woman by keeping her locked inside their outhouse for the nine months of her pregnancy, feeding her very scarcely. Due to this malnutrition, her baby was very frail after birth and only lived to be two months of age.

Despite this scandalous event, Mrs. Otto maintained the servants at her home, giving the foreign woman her predetermined role as nanny. Regardless of the past, the

Ghost Stories

woman took good care of young Robert Eugene and grew incredibly fond of him, treating him as if he was her own son.

The situation at the household seemed normal for a while, and things appeared to move along in a regular fashion. This was until a certain incident made Mrs. Otto furious, ultimately leading her to banish her four servants. On one occasion, she went outside during the night and stumbled upon a frightening scene. She witnessed her servants carrying out a ritual that was an established custom in the Santeria religion. This faith incorporates elements of voodoo and animal sacrifice. They were slaughtering a chicken as their offering in the course of this ritual.

Mrs. Otto was repulsed and ordered her servants to leave the premises the first thing in the morning. Since she had become very attached to young Otto, the nanny tried to convince her mistress not to separate them, but her efforts were futile. As a farewell gift, the Bahamian woman made a doll for the young boy, and he was allowed to keep it as his toy.

Hannah J. Tidy

Whichever of the two stories is true, the gifting of this doll to Robert Eugene marked the beginning of the horrors and hauntings that were to follow for years and years.

From that point on, the young boy became incredibly attached to his doll, and people would routinely see him taking it along when playing outside or walking the streets, all the while talking to the doll. The first signs that there might have been something strange about Eugene's doll were rather innocuous and could have been ascribed to simply the child's shenanigans. Household items and various objects would sometimes be thrown around the place or broken. Naturally, the parents would put the blame on their son and reprimand him. However, the boy would always point to the doll and say that it was the doll that did it. More disturbingly, however, Eugene also began to be irritated when his parents referred to him by his full name and would warn them not to call him Robert Eugene Otto. Instead, he wanted to be called Eugene or Gene (otherwise his nickname), while his first name was reserved for his supposedly inanimate companion. "It wasn't me, Robert did it!" became something of a standard thing for Eugene to say when accused of any wrongdoing.

Ghost Stories

The boy would sometimes also have nightmares and get loud and restless in his sleep. His parents would then enter the room with haste to see what happened, only to be greeted by a scene where furniture and other items were shoved about and displaced. "It was Robert," Eugene would always explain, pointing at the doll. As some stories suggest, his parents claimed that they would sometimes hear the doll chuckle, and even move around the house.

Strange incidents continued through the years, and Eugene never let go of Robert. Even in early adulthood, at around age nineteen, people would still see him taking the doll with him down the street, talking to it. According to some sources, this was also the time when his parents decided to move to France, leaving Robert behind, locked in a wooden chest in the attic.

Without Robert, Eugene lived a healthy and reasonably fulfilling life, and he even got married. Later on, he decided to move back to his house in Florida with his wife, Ann, and make a life in his childhood home. As the story goes, Eugene completely forgot almost everything about Robert the Doll, especially the chest where they left him prior to moving.

Upon finding him, the past began to flood back into his life, and he found himself inseparable from Robert once again. His peculiar behavior, such as taking the doll with him outside and talking to it, was hardly becoming of a grown, married man. He quickly got a reputation as an eccentric, wacky artist. Eugene's wife was especially troubled by his behavior, and he was ultimately forced to keep Robert strictly in the dome area, above the second story of his house.

Eugene's strange conduct continued, and he allegedly began to have violent outbursts against his wife as well and became an abusive man overall. At one point, he even locked Ann in the old outhouse for three days. When she got out, he put the blame on Robert, just like he would back when he was a little boy. He subsequently proclaimed Robert the head of the house, built furniture for him, and even demanded that he be fed regularly, before anybody else. Other people who visited the Otto home would sometimes report hearing steps upstairs as if the doll was walking around. Ann frequently heard Eugene talk to his doll when he was alone with it, at times even sounding as if Robert was hurting him and Gene was begging him to stop.

Ghost Stories

Further reports came from children who'd walk past the house on their way to school or home. They reported seeing the doll appear and then vanish from the windows in the dome top of the Artist House, moving around the attic as if it were alive. Many of them grew afraid of the house and would steer well clear of it, while other children perceived it as something of an attraction in the neighborhood.

After years and years of this horror, Eugene passed away in 1974. Some stories suggest that even Eugene's death was bizarre. In particular, it is said that he was found dead in the attic of the house, which was by now the quarters designated entirely as Robert's dwelling. Freakily enough, Robert was supposedly on top of Eugene's body, with his hands around his neck. Soon after that, Ann decided to sell the house and move back to her homeland, leaving both Roberts behind.

One would assume that there must be a great deal of exaggeration in these stories or at least some of them. Or perhaps, there could be some explanation, if you disregard a lot of the reports and testimonies. Could it be that Eugene suffered from severe mental problems from a very young age? At times, some of the stories definitely point to a level of insanity plaguing this man. Some occurrences resemble symptoms of a multiple personality disorder, in particular. However, other than the fact that so many stories cropped up during Eugene's lifetime, there is one more factor to consider when contemplating the legitimacy of the legend. This factor is one simple fact – the story doesn't end with Eugene.

That's right. The cursed doll was nowhere near finished with the people around it. It wasn't long after Eugene's death that the new owner of the house, Myrtle Reuter, settled in with her young daughter. Naturally, curious as a child always is, the girl soon came across Robert the Doll, who was left collecting dust in his attic domicile. The story has it that the little girl quickly became acquainted with the curse that Robert had carried. She reported that he tormented her in different ways and that he was trying to hurt her. Just like before, people who came to the house sometimes reported strange noises coming from the attic, and Myrtle Reuter took notice as well and believed that she heard the doll move around the house. After quite a while of putting up with small-scale paranormal incidents and unpleasantness,

Ghost Stories

Reuters decided to get rid of the doll, and she donated it to the local museum in 1994.

As he had already become something of an urban legend by then, he attracted scores of people from all over to come and see him with their own eyes. Believers, skeptics, as well as various enthusiasts, visit Robert to this day. Furthermore, he regularly gets letters from those who have and would love to visit him alike. Interestingly enough, some of those letters are apologies from former skeptics who didn't believe but apparently found themselves under an avalanche of misfortune after their visit. This is especially the case with those who disrespected him in different ways. According to many, there is one thing that the cursed doll sees as a particular kind of disrespect, and that's taking pictures of it without permission. As silly as it sounds, there have been letters sent to the museum in which people apologized for photographing him, since their life went completely downhill after the fact, leaving them feeling cursed. The misfortunes reported include divorces, deaths of loved ones, financial ruin, car accidents, and other mishaps that may befall anybody. There is even a warning sign at the museum, urging visitors not to photograph Robert. As can be

Hannah J. Tidy

expected, there are also letters sent by people asking for life advice, or for Robert to curse their enemies and rivals.

While the replies that are sometimes sent via mail or email come from the museum employees, the curse that has been perceived by many certainly doesn't. Whether the voodoo spell that has enchanted Robert the Doll with evil powers is real or not, his exhibition in the museum has certainly captivated a lot of people and cemented his legend and popularity like never before.

Ghost Stories

Chapter -12

Hauntings – Annabelle

Another Hardly Amusing Toy

If that was your first time hearing about Robert the Doll, then perhaps you might have heard of Annabelle before. Arguably more famous than Robert's, the story of Annabelle is yet another terrifying collection of accounts and legends revolving around a peculiar doll, although "peculiar" doesn't even come close to doing her justice.

Just like Robert, Annabelle was an inspiration for an array of horror movies, particularly "The Conjuring," and "Annabelle" from 2014, and its 2017 sequel. Annabelle is a doll made after Raggedy Ann, who was a female character in a children's picture book series that started in 1918 in the

US, with dolls entering production a couple of years prior. The doll itself may come across as fairly creepy, depending on how you perceive it, especially when you know the story behind it. Objectively, however, there is nothing particularly striking about its appearance, it's a regular toy doll, created in the fashion of its time. It is around a foot in height, has two large, round eyes with dilated pupils, a triangular nose, and is wearing an old-fashioned, white nightdress.

The legend of the haunted Annabelle doll is also a more recent tale, as it starts around the year 1970. A girl named Donna, who was studying to become a nurse at the time, was given Annabelle as a birthday present that year by her mother. Reportedly, the doll was something of an antique and was bought pre-loved at a store. Donna lived with a roommate by the name of Angie, who also studied for the same profession in college. The two young women lived in a small apartment that they rented out together.

Most of what we know about the supposedly possessed Annabelle comes from the Warren couple, Ed, and Lorraine, who are famous for their investigations into the paranormal, or anything pertaining to hauntings, ghosts, demons, etc.

There were a couple of other accounts as well, though, such as that of the girls, as well as Lou, who was friends with the two women who kept the doll at their apartment.

As the story has it, those who came into contact with Annabelle on a regular basis would swear that the doll moved around on its own, sometimes had what appeared to be blood stains on its hands or dress, and even left written messages! These letters would read, "Help us." or "Help Lou." In the early stages of the ordeal, though, the perceived incidents would be much milder. Donna and Angie would often come back home, confident of where they had last left her, to find that Annabelle had moved to a different place or even completely migrated outside of the room she was left in.

In a particularly terrifying episode, it's said that Donna returned home and saw that Annabelle had moved onto her bed. As strange as it may sound, she had grown somewhat accustomed to the quirkiness surrounding her doll and didn't take the possibility of her actually moving around too seriously. However, on this particular occasion, upon further inspection, she discovered what appeared to be droplets of blood, or at least a similar substance, both on her hands and her body. This time, Donna was quite distraught by what she had seen, and she got in contact with whom she thought was the most appropriate – a medium to the spiritual realm. So, she scheduled a session in the hopes of obtaining some answers.

The medium attempted to establish communication with any spirits that may have potentially been lurking in or around the doll. According to what the medium discovered, the ghost of a girl called Annabelle Higgins possessed the doll. This girl was allegedly found dead at only seven years of age, right on the grounds where the residential building that Donna lived in was built. Furthermore, Donna was told that the spirit of the little girl not only wanted to live on through the doll but also to be taken care of and nurtured by Donna and her roommate. Donna was touched by the story, and she decided that she could live with this and keep Annabelle.

Since the very beginning, when Donna first received Annabelle from her mother, Lou objected that the thing had a malicious nature about it, and he advised Donna to do

Ghost Stories

away with it and just throw it out. However, Donna grew rather fond of the doll and became attached to it, so she paid little heed to what her friend was saying. She especially wanted to keep it after the medium told her the story about the Higgins girl.

It wasn't long until Lou began to have his own paranormal run-ins with Annabelle. It started with him having recurring nightmares, haunted by Annabelle in various ways. One especially horrifying experience he had with the doll was when he woke up in the middle of the night from another one of his nightly terrors. He found himself unable to move whatsoever. All he could do was look around the room while having a feeling of terrible dread. He didn't see anything at first, but when he looked down his body, he saw Annabelle at his feet. She crawled along his legs and got to his chest, where she began to strangle him. Still, he was completely helpless and unable to move, as the doll was suffocating him. Panicking and struggling to draw a breath, Lou passed out at that point. When he woke up in the morning, he remained confident that this was no dream.

Hannah J. Tidy

If you are familiar with the phenomenon of sleep paralysis, you probably think that Lou's experience has a lot in common with the stories of people who have experienced the same. Hallucinations, horror, and asphyxiation are common in all the reports. It's certainly logical to assume that this was what Lou had experienced, especially if this was his only direct contact with the possessed doll. It wasn't.

For instance, the stories also say that Lou and Angie, some time later were alone in their apartment going over their plans for an upcoming road trip and mapping out their route. The silence that kept them company until then was suddenly interrupted by unusual noises coming from the room belonging to Donna, who was out at this time. Lou decided to investigate, and he slowly snuck his way up to the door, listening in without going inside at first. When the noise stopped, he barged in and found nothing out of the ordinary except the doll, which was in the corner of the room.

He inspected the room thoroughly for any signs of a break-in, but nothing seemed broken, misplaced, or tampered with in any way. However, a strange feeling came over him as soon as he stepped closer to Annabelle, and he felt inclined to check if someone was behind him. As soon as he turned around, he was shocked by a pain in his chest, and he realized that he was slashed across his chest area, bleeding. He saw blood on his shirt and a few cuts that appeared as if they were inflicted by claws. Allegedly, these slash marks healed right away and were completely gone within the next two days.

This incident led them to seek help once again, and even Donna began to suspect that, if truly possessed, Annabelle was much more malicious than she was led to believe. She started thinking that there is an evil presence within Annabelle, and not the ghost of a girl who just wanted to be cuddled and cared for.

Soon after that, she sought help from a priest who forwarded the report to one of his superiors, Father Cooke. Cooke got in touch with the couple Ed and Lorraine Warren, the paranormal investigators mentioned earlier. The Warrens established contact with Donna soon after that, and they discussed the details of the case and all its incidents. Based on their experience in dealing with the paranormal, they explained what they felt was actually happening with Annabelle. They told Donna that struggling human spirits generally don't possess objects. Instead, they wander and haunt wider locations, but when they possess, they possess people in particular. Furthermore, they said that what was at play here was an inhuman spirit, a demonic presence, as these forces are what can take hold of an object. The cruel spirits use this as a temporary solution in their process of finding a human soul to take hold of. In this case, the soul that this demon coveted was Donna's.

The Warrens scheduled a time for their visit to Donna's apartment, and Father Cooke went along too. At the scene, he agreed with the Warrens to perform an exorcism ritual in an attempt to banish the demonic spirit from the apartment and, hopefully, the doll itself. The exorcism was conducted through the proper rites and recitations. Still, the Warrens asked Donna to let go of the doll and let them take it just in case the exorcism didn't work. Donna agreed, and this was the time when the Warrens first took possession of the troublesome toy.

Ghost Stories

They brought it with them and, according to the Warrens, took precautions for their own safety, such as avoiding the highway on their way home. As they further told, their suspicions proved right, and the doll continued to be possessed by the dark force. The couple reported having minor but strange problems with their car not long after they departed.

The doll was taken to the Warren household, which is where they intended to keep it. However, they reported that Annabelle brought strange happenings to their home, in much of the same ways that she did while Donna kept her. At one point, they brought in another priest and asked him to attempt an exorcism on Annabelle, which he did. Reportedly, the priest took the supposedly possessed doll less than seriously despite Ed's warnings. On his way home, however, the priest lost control of his car and went straight into a busy intersection, totaling his vehicle and putting him within the edge of his life. Lorraine said that she warned him to drive carefully on his way home, only to receive a call, later on, informing her of what had transpired. As for the exorcism, it didn't seem to have had any long-lasting effects.

Ultimately, the Warrens decided to confine the haunted doll once and for all. A special glass case was built, with a roof and a cross on top, resembling a church. This case houses Annabelle in the Warrens Occult Museum, in Monroe, Connecticut, which the couple manage. There is also a warning sign on the case that reads, "Warning, positively do not open."

Along with numerous other trophies and artifacts that the Warrens collected in their line of work dealing with the paranormal, Annabelle is there on display, and she can be seen by visitors from all over. If you happen to visit the Occult Museum one day, tread lightly, regardless of whether or not you believe the legend as told by the Warrens. There is a story of a particularly skeptical young man, who was very confident and outspoken in his disbelief of Annabelle's haunting. He allegedly demanded from Ed for the doll to cut him just as the doll had cut Lou, but nothing happened.

The young man then left with his girlfriend on their motorcycle. The girl later said that they were laughing about the story when the motorcycle spiraled out of control and

Ghost Stories

they crashed into a tree, leaving the man dead at the scene and landing the young woman in the hospital.

Of course, stories as freaky as this should always be taken with a healthy dose of skepticism, and everybody is right to do so. However, it is perhaps best not to push one's luck and challenge the unseen forces that may well exist; forces that we do not understand.

Hannah J. Tidy

Chapter -13

Hauntings – Doris Bither

The Horror behind the Horror

If you're a fan of horror flicks, the chances are that you have heard of 1982's "The Entity." This was a horror film that many are unaware was based on true events. In the chilling story, a paranormal force that turns out to be a demon of some sort sexually assaults a woman. The movie was based on a book of the same name, written in the late 1970s, which, in turn, took after the alleged haunting that befell Doris Bither, starting early in the same decade, in Culver City, California.

As was later revealed by investigators who handled Doris' case from 1974, the woman had lived a life of hardship and abuse long before supernatural torment was upon her too.

At a very young age, Doris was forced out of her home and had to make her own way the best she could. She had also been involved in numerous dysfunctional relationships with men all her life, with a lot of them turning abusive. Doris also brought additional trouble on herself in adolescence, as she began to gain an interest in ghosts and would often attempt to spawn them via Ouija boards and other methods.

After years of trials and tribulations, Doris eventually fell into substance abuse, which persisted for most of her life, especially when it came to drinking. This fact, as well as her deep emotional scars, contributed to the arguments made by many skeptics later on, which believed Doris wasn't of exactly sound mind. However, Doris was far from alone in witnessing the hauntings, especially after investigators became involved.

The case, which at first appeared to be a regular instance of haunting, piqued the interest of renowned parapsychologist and paranormal investigator Dr. Barry Taff. In the summer of 1974, Taff and an associate of his, Kerry Gaynor, were at a bookstore, engaged in conversation on the topic of paranormal phenomena. It was then that Doris Bither, who

Ghost Stories

walked up to them that she believed her house was haunted and that she'd like them to investigate it, overheard them. The details she provided intrigued the investigators, but they weren't told the whole story at that time. The interest was enough to motivate a visit, though, and they went to her house on August 22.

When they arrived, they took note of the rather poor living conditions in the neglected home. Doris, a single mother, had four children from four different fathers living with her in the house. At the time, Doris' daughter was only six, and her three sons were aged ten, thirteen, and sixteen. It was also apparent to Taff and Gaynor that the mother had a strained relationship with her male children, especially the teens.

The investigators started by conducting an interview with Doris, which went on for a couple of hours, as Doris described various anomalies her family had experienced in the house. There was allegedly much of the usual activity associated with poltergeists, but some particularly disturbing details included her and the children actually bumping into ghosts. As Dr. Taff later explained in an

137

interview he gave on television, he couldn't shake the feeling that Doris was omitting an important aspect of the story while they talked.

Ultimately, however, Doris opened up, and the story turned into a whole new shade of disturbing and vile. She explained that there were three ghosts, in particular, whom she described as Asian men, who would not only hunt her but actually rape her. The trio consisted of two smaller specters that would restrain her with invisible and overwhelming force, while a third, larger poltergeist assaulted her. She also mentioned one instance where her oldest son tried to defend her but was subdued and thrown away by the invisible assailants, causing an arm injury on the boy. As for the very existence of these entities, it was supported by testimonies from neighbors, who claimed to have indeed seen apparitions around Doris' home.

When it came to the alleged rape, Doris herself presented some evidence to the investigators. They spoke of Doris showing them severe bruising on her inner thighs and several other places on her body. It appeared as though these ghosts were almost a regular occurrence around the home,

Ghost Stories

as the children were all aware of their existence. One of the ghosts even earned a nickname of "Mr. Whose-It" from the kids.

Barry Taff heard out Doris' story and was hooked, but he was highly skeptical of certain aspects of it, especially the allegations of spectral rape. This was the first time he and Gaynor heard such a thing from a victim of a haunting. Regardless, Taff and Gaynor decided to summon their team to the house and set up their equipment in the hopes of detecting and possibly capturing any paranormal evidence.

All told, after Taff made the calls, there were around thirty investigators on location, including photographers and the like. They then told Doris to try and summon her spectral tormentors, which she did by calling and cursing them. Surely enough, as the witnesses told, orbs and arcs of light started to materialize in the room. The team started taking photographs and recording the phenomena, but capturing anything clear proved rather difficult because the lights were very difficult to frame. In particular, as Taff explained in a later interview, each time they snapped a photo, the developed photographs turned out almost completely white, obviously blinded by some sort of flash.

He showed these photographs in the same interview, including a couple of pictures that actually succeeded in catching an arc of light across the photo. In one of the pictures he presented, a corner can be seen in the background with the arc spanning across without bending, proving that it wasn't light from a flashlight being projected onto the wall. The bright white arc in this black and white picture can be seen encircling Doris from overhead, as she sits on the bed in said corner.

This interference with the cameras also occurred when they tried to photograph what Doris was insisting was a ghost. She kept pointing at something she said she was seeing, but nobody else noticed anything. Doris would frantically yell that "it" was right in front of her face. Barry explained that they tried to capture whatever it might have been with their Polaroid instant cameras, again getting flashed out pictures. Curiously enough, Barry got the idea to take photos when Doris was not close by and compare the results. Surely enough, the pictures taken when Doris wasn't around were

Ghost Stories

perfectly normal. All the while, pungent, disgusting smells would emit randomly from different sources, usually coming from where Doris would point.

Amid these confrontations, the team also described a mysterious green mist that started to emerge in one of the corners, spreading upwards and ultimately forming what looked like a silhouette of a male torso that came across as quite muscular. Upon seeing this, one member of the team reportedly fainted.

The team spent a couple of months observing and documenting what Barry Taff described as a "plethora of phenomena during the investigation." The anomalies decreased in intensity and frequency as time went by.

There were a few very important facts about Doris that related to the case and the possible explanations thereof. Barry Taff put a lot of effort into trying to explain what was happening, and he has developed some interesting theories in that regard.

First of all, as we've mentioned, Doris had a drinking problem, which she refused to properly address all her life. This was her way of living with the figurative demons within,

141

birthed from so much trauma that she had endured in life. Her childhood was a reel of abuse and hardship, which left some very deep scars in her soul. Things just kept getting worse as she entered adulthood and got involved in relationships. After all, she had four children, none of whose fathers were around to help. Due to her emotional problems and possible mistrust towards men, her relationship with her sons was dysfunctional, to say the least.

Taff stated that all of this played a crucial part in the hauntings. First and foremost, Taff remained skeptical of the concept of "spectral rape" to the very end. He didn't dismiss that Doris had been attacked by the poltergeists, but he offered his own theory as to what exactly was at work. It appeared, he noted, that the paranormal activity would start and be most intense around Doris when she was under the influence, whereas things would usually be completely normal when she was sober.

Barry Taff further explained that he believed these poltergeists were psychosomatic – manifestations of Doris' inner turmoil and emotional baggage, such as rage, pain, depression, addiction, etc. More importantly, however, he expressed his belief that Doris had psychokinetic powers, which, when combined with her inner demons and negative energy, especially when unhinged during an alcoholic stupor, resulted in those demons manifesting themselves onto the physical world. This meant they affected her directly as well, which, Barry explains, resulted in Doris believing she was raped. He saw this assault as a projection of Doris' suppressed trauma and experiences of abuse, as well as the toxic energy between her and the three boys she was raising, which does resemble Doris' account of precisely three spectral assailants.

Furthermore, some believe that psychokinetic powers are hereditary. Therefore, it could be theorized that her sons and their own negative feelings towards Doris, her neglect, and her addiction, channeled even more power into the pool of paranormal energy and anomalous activity in the household. If the family indeed possessed psychokinetic powers, it's also possible that the three ghosts were physical figments of the minds of her sons themselves, who thus inadvertently projected their anger onto the mother with terrifying, supernatural results. These paranormal attacks could have triggered memories and were then, in turn, perceived by drunken Doris as rape, since there is a good possibility that she had lived through sexual assault sometime during her life.

Essentially, what all of this means is that Dr. Taff believed that Doris herself could have been the source of the phenomena surrounding her. The psychokinetic power of her mind channeled the contents of her subconscious mind right into the real world, without her even knowing it, let alone being able to control it. Barry Taff didn't claim this as the ultimate truth, nor did he state that he had irrefutable answers, but he feels that this compelling possibility appealed the most to the fascinating case of Doris Bither.

There is one final detail that corroborates this theory of his. Namely, the phenomena reportedly ceased in the house after Doris left, and no subsequent residents reported anything strange. Doris moved a couple of times throughout California, went to Texas at one point, and eventually settled in San Bernardino. However, she reported that her ghostly persecutors followed her everywhere she went. If this was indeed the case, then it is a very strong indication that Taff was right.

Ghost Stories

Whatever the precise case was, the life of Doris Bither was a jagged string of hardship and misfortune. Her apparent confrontation with the forces beyond only added to the suffering. Regardless, the fact that she sought help from Barry Taff and Kerry Gaynor showed that she did have a will to fight her demons, and it also gave Taff one of the most fascinating cases among thousands he has investigated to date. The case stays with him to this day and continues to haunt all those who were involved with it. As for Doris, one of her sons has reported that she had died back in 1999, at the age of only fifty-nine, due to respiratory complications. Whatever waits for us beyond our realm after we pass, we can only hope that Doris has finally found peace from both the figurative and actual ghosts that had haunted her for all her life. If the unfortunate can't find solace and refuge in this life, it's pleasant to imagine that it at least comes after we're put to rest.

Hannah J. Tidy

Chapter -14

Hauntings - The Cecil Hotel

Elisa Lam Tapes And More

We've taken a look at a haunted painting, and now we are moving on to something with even more history and layers of gore - The Cecil Hotel. There are so many strange and horrifying stories surrounding this hotel that it can undoubtedly be classified as "certifiably haunted."

In the 1920's, Los Angeles was a bustling place. Business was booming, and Hollywood was taking shape. Los Angeles was now the 5th largest city in the United States, and its port was second only to New York City. It is only understandable that hotels were in an incredibly high demand. The Cecil Hotel was constructed in 1924 with an astonishing 700 rooms and

Hannah J. Tidy

was meant to house a large number of business travelers that were coming into and going out of the city.

While Los Angeles was able to survive through the Great Depression in the 1930's and WWII in the 1940's, the effects of the economic downturn and the war took a toll on the real estate industry. This change in the property market led to an entirely different clientele for the Cecil Hotel. With an increase in wealth disparity, a need for a resting place for transients became more and more necessary, and the Cecil Hotel filled the void. The low prices allowed people to have a temporary home out of the small rooms the hotel offered. The business model eventually transitioned to long-term single room leases where tenants shared the hallway bathrooms.

It was during this time that the Cecil Hotel began taking on a sinister nature. It started to develop a reputation for suicides. People would come to the hotel, climb its 14 stories, and jump out of windows to their death. There are at least three documented cases of suicides.

What the Cecil Hotel became even more known for was the notoriety of two of its tenants – serial killers both. The first

Ghost Stories

of the two serial killers was Texas born Richard Ramirez. He became known as the "Night Stalker" in the 1980s due to his ability to stalk and kill his victims at night. His life changed dramatically when he was forced to watch his cousin Mike, who had become a role model to him, shoot Mike's wife in front of Ramirez' eyes. Mike was a Vietnam Veteran and had no qualms about sharing his sexual and murderous exploits in Vietnam with his younger cousin, Richard. Ramirez then developed an appetite for sexual fantasies that included violence and bondage and was committing crimes even in Junior High. He dropped out of school before finishing 9th grade and moved to California, where his career as a serial killer would begin. He went on to commit numerous burglaries and at least 13 murders; with several more attempted murders. The majority of his crimes took place in LA in July and August of 1985, with some murders occurring only days apart from each other. It was during this time that it is believed he lived at the Cecil Hotel.

The second serial killer to live in the hotel was Jack Unterweger. Unterweger began his crimes in Europe and later came to the United States. He was known for targeting prostitutes. The Cecil Hotel served as the perfect place for him to take residence in LA, due to its reputation of housing poor and low-class people. He killed a total of three prostitutes while living there and supposedly stayed there in homage to Ramirez.

With all of this history of bloodshed, it is no wonder that the Cecil Hotel developed quite the reputation for being haunted. The ghosts of dozens of victims and lost souls wander the halls at night, and guests that stay there often report feeling a lost and depressed presence.

In 2007, the Cecil Hotel was taken over by new management, refurbished and rebranded as "Stay On Main." The Lanting Hotel Group reopened it as a combination hotel/youth hostel, with both hotel rooms and transient rooms to be rented out on a semi-permanent basis. However, this rebranding did nothing to rid the house of its evil spirits.

In 2013, the hotel was brought back into the limelight with the mysterious case of Elisa Lam. Elisa was a student from Vancouver, Canada, who was staying at the hotel during her visit to Los Angeles. She was later reported missing, and soon after, a video clip taken from CCTV footage of the

Ghost Stories

elevator of the hotel surfaced. It was the last anyone had heard from Elisa. It showed her going in and out of the elevator and motioning in a strange and unnatural way with her hands. A few days after she was reported missing, other guests in the hotel started to complain of issues in the quality of their water. This led to the servicing of the water tank on the top of the high-rise building. What they found there shocked everyone. Elisa Lam was found floating, stark naked with her clothes strewn all around her, very much dead in the water. She had been decomposing in the water tank for a week before being found.

The autopsy showed nothing to go on with - no drugs, no alcohol, no evidence of foul play - and thus, authorities ruled it a suicide. But why would a perfectly happy girl on the vacation trip of her lifetime all of a sudden decide to commit suicide? The answer is simple; she was murdered. But the killer may not have been someone you'd suspect. Could it be that the same evil ghosts who have haunted the hotel for decades, for some reason, led Elisa Lam to this tragic and horrific end?

Hannah J. Tidy

The question is, did all these gruesome events stop business at the hotel? On the contrary, "Stay on Main" has become more popular than ever, and is well on its way to its 100th anniversary. As an added attraction, psychics who claim they are able to connect with the spirits residing there offer 'special tours' of the hotel for the hauntingly inclined. The hotel's sordid history has sparked a whole slew of conspiracy theories and paranormal explanations that, until this day, keep horror aficionados up all night. Elisa Lam's story has also sparked a whole slew of new entertainment in the form of movies and literature.

If you want to stay at the hotel, you can do so for $45, if you are willing to share a room with another traveler. This is a great price for the downtown location that "Stay on Main" offers. Knowing the history of the hotel, you might actually prefer sleeping with someone else as opposed to being alone. Of course, private rooms are also available, but they cost a little more at $75. A Private Room with a unique ghost visitor sounds like a hauntingly good deal for the truly brave of heart.

Ghost Stories

Chapter -15

Hauntings – Amityville

The House of Terror

The story of the haunted house in Amityville, New York, is one of the most publicized cases involving the Warren couple and their paranormal investigations. It has spawned and inspired a few famous movies, such as the 1979's "The Amityville Horror" and the 2005 remake. This fame and the exaggerations characteristic of Hollywood may be a few of the reasons why it is also one of the most challenged and questioned of the Warrens' stories. Or perhaps, the fact that it is arguably the most fascinating one breeds both the controversy and the popularity. Then again, there's hardly a story of a ghost sighting or a haunting in the world that has not been suspected and met with a lot of skepticism. Either

Hannah J. Tidy

way, it is quite a frightening tale of a haunted place. A place already cursed with so much evil that was documented to have transpired on the premises. This dark history has certainly left it's mark on the suburban house in Amityville; the only question is, whether or not this maliciousness lives on through something more than just a memory of human darkness.

This talk of darkness and evil refers to a bloodbath that happened within the house in November of 1974, around a year before the Lutz family moved in. Ronald DeFeo Jr. murdered his entire family in cold blood, including both of his parents, his two brothers, and two sisters. The victims had been executed in their beds during the night, with a rifle. DeFeo tried to mask his atrocity by going to the local bar and "looking for help," proclaiming that his parents had been murdered. The ammunition used in the killings was soon found in DeFeo's possession by the police, and he was subsequently arrested. He further explained that he didn't even know that his siblings had been killed too when he went to the bar to "look for help." He said that the only victims that he found in the house were his parents.

Ghost Stories

All these accounts of DeFeo were, as far as everybody was concerned, complete lies, and he was found guilty of six counts of second-degree murder. For his harrowing crimes, he was given six sentences of twenty-five years to life, which he still serves.

However, DeFeo gave varying stories and testimonies as to what exactly happened at the house. His defense attorney attempted to get an insanity ruling, claiming that DeFeo was hearing voices in his head that told him to commit the crime. Overall, he was rather inconsistent, blaming his sister and even an outside perpetrator at times. All of these allegations were disregarded as fabrications, and his sentences continued to stand. It's safe to assume that he did, in fact, murder his family, but some of the particulars of the case are indeed peculiar. Namely, every single one of the six victims was found in bed, face down. One would expect that the rest of the family would take notice as soon as Ronald fired the first shot, but the positions that the bodies were found in suggest that they didn't react at all. The police investigators were troubled by the same speculations in the beginning. How could one man move so fast and execute six people in their beds before any one of them woke up from the noise and checked to see what was going on in the house? One possible explanation was that the family was sedated or otherwise drugged into a deep sleep, but toxicology results refuted this theory. Furthermore, it's particularly strange that no neighbor reported hearing any gunfire, and the police did confirm that the weapon he used was not suppressed.

Whatever the curious details of that night may be, DeFeo was found guilty of the crime, and that horrifying event is believed to be the cause of the alleged haunting of the house by evil spirits.

As the story goes, the Lutz family moved into the house just a little over a year after the murders. They were aware of the horrendous, recent past that plagued the home, but they were fond of the house's Dutch colonial style, and the price was rather appealing to them. The Lutz family included George and Kathy, and three children from Kathy's previous marriage: Daniel, Missy, and Christopher.

On the very day that they moved in, Kathy requested that a Catholic priest be invited to bless their new home, which was easily arranged. It was at this time that the first paranormal

Ghost Stories

reports began to start. While the priest was blessing the house and using his holy water throughout the house, he went into the room that was previously used by two of the DeFeo boys, Marc and John. It was alleged that the priest heard a deep, unsettling voice talk directly to him, warning him to leave the house. The priest complied, but he didn't tell the family exactly what he experienced. Instead, he simply left them with an ominous warning not to use that room for sleeping under any circumstance. They decided to take his advice and designated the room for their sewing machine.

Some time later, in 1979, a television show called "In Search of," supposedly tracked down the priest in question and invited him to give an interview on the program. The priest agreed, but he demanded that he wanted to remain anonymous, so his face was kept hidden in the program.

The man described the experience in his own words, explaining that the room felt strange from the moment he walked in. He said it was much colder than one would expect, and that the voice talked to him as he started sprinkling his holy water. The supposed priest quoted the demonic voice as simply saying "Get out!" Furthermore, he described a physical sensation right after that. This sensation was in the form of a slap on his face, despite the fact that he was completely alone in the room. In the interview, he also mentioned that he allegedly began having cysts or blisters appear on his hands shortly after that incident.

The show's episode also went on to share how the priest tried to call the family later on, to warn and inform them of the full scope of the evil threat in their house. However, there seemed to be something always wrong with the phone connection, and unyielding static interference prevented any clear communication.

After the priest left and the family finished unpacking and settling in, the trouble began to start that very night within the household. From that moment on when they officially moved in, many aspects of their life began to deteriorate for the Lutz family. At first, they experienced all kinds of strange feelings; both physical and mental. They all became more irritable and uneasy, leading to tension and arguments in the home. George talked about how he could never seem to

Ghost Stories

warm up, feeling a persistent cold in his bones when he was at home, regardless of how much he tried to keep the fire strong and raise the temperature in the house. These random, cold areas within the house were mentioned by Daniel too, and most of the other people involved in these incidents. The couple also said that even their physical health began to worsen over time.

Their young daughter, Missy, started to behave in a particularly quirky way as well. She became something of a shut-in and spent a lot of time in her room all alone, at least as far as anybody else thought. Missy claimed that she was not alone and that she had a friend called Jodie who hung around with her most of the time. Of course, everyone else perceived Jodie as an imaginary friend of Missy's, which is a relatively typical occurrence with certain young children. Missy described Jodie in different ways at times, most notably as a pig with glowing, red eyes and as an angel-type being. Supposedly, Jodie could shape-shift and change her appearance and size, and it is said that Missy described Jodie as sometimes being enormous, bigger than their house even. She also explained that Jodie only made herself visible

159

to whom she wanted, while being completely invisible otherwise.

Although other members of the family see Jodie in some parts of the Amityville movies, nobody reported seeing her in real life. If you saw the movies, you'll also perhaps remember the onslaught of massive swarms of flies in the house. Members of the family were asked whether this happened in their experience or not. "Inside Edition" conducted an interview in 2005 where this was inquired. Christopher and Daniel both said that there was, indeed, an unusual number of flies at their home, particularly in the sewing room. However, Chris stated that the movies greatly exaggerated the amount.

The family also spoke of strange, highly unpleasant smells that would start spreading at random, with their source remaining a mystery. George Lutz also talked about black spots appearing on the ceramics in their bathroom and their toilet bowl apparently turning black. There were also reports of peculiar substances of unknown origin appearing at different locations in the home, although there was never any blood trickling down the walls like in the movie, which

Ghost Stories

was confirmed by George as well. Furthermore, much like the priest's experience where he felt like some mysterious force slapped him, Kathy also talked about apparent physical contact, where she was allegedly touched by someone or something that she could not see.

There were a few other things in the Amityville movie that have been confirmed as true by the Lutz family. Namely, Daniel confirmed that a window did smash into his hand at one point, one of his fingers is still somewhat bent up to the present because of the injury he sustained. Christopher explained, later on, that the windows in the house would often open and shut on their own, although none of them ever broke. The infamous red room exists in reality too, although it may have been over-dramatized on screen. In particular, the red room refers to a small storage compartment under the stairs, leading into the basement.

According to some of his accounts, George woke up to a hair-raising sight on one particular night. His wife Kathy appeared to have changed into a frightening old hag, which horrified him. George would often wake up in the middle of the night and generally had many sleepless nights too. As a matter of fact, Lutz claimed that he would routinely wake up at precisely 3:15 in the morning on a daily basis, which is believed to be around the time when DeFeo committed the murders. On another occasion, he said that he even saw his wife levitating above their bed, after which he heard loud noises coming from his children's rooms as if their beds were being moved around with force. When he wanted to go and investigate what was going on, he found himself paralyzed in bed, unable to lift a single finger.

It's also said that the family attempted to get in touch with the priest who blessed the house a few times, in order to seek his help. However, the phone would always seem to experience technical problems when they tried to talk to him. Allegedly, when they tried to banish the spirits with their own crucifix, they were told by otherworldly voices to stop what they were doing immediately.

The night that pushed the family over the edge was particularly shocking, as the Lutz family shared. There were incredibly loud noises everywhere in the house; furniture was being moved and tossed around frantically, terrifying the couple and the children. They decided that they wouldn't

Ghost Stories

take it anymore. It took only twenty-eight days for the Lutz family to choose to evacuate from the premises and they temporarily stayed with Kathy's mother. George later told of the horrors they experienced, and he said that it might have been this evil presence that pushed Ronald DeFeo to murder his family. This possibility made him more sympathetic towards the murderer, and he believed that his insanity plea might have actually been founded in truth. Despite this, DeFeo later admitted that all his talk of voices commanding him to kill were fabrications and part of his attempt to be acquitted by reason of insanity.

Some twenty days after the Lutz family ran from the house, a reporter who was working on the story decided to call in the Warren couple to help with the investigation. They brought in a team with them as well, but the Lutz family, the Warrens claimed, would not enter the house again during the investigations.

Ed Warren said that he was actually knocked down on the floor by an unseen force in the basement, and his wife talked about positively feeling an incredibly evil presence in the house – a presence that was of a demonic nature. In the course of their investigations, the Warrens found that, before the house was built in 1924, the land belonged to one John Ketchum, who was involved in black magic and requested that he be buried on the grounds after his death.

A different investigation involved a medium at the house, who claimed that he managed to establish contact with the spirit of an old Indian chief, who was tormenting all who resided on the premises. His reason for this, the medium explained, was anger over the fact that this was an old Indian burial ground. However, the natives of the Montaukett tribe still living on Long Island spoke out against this theory, explaining that they had no written record of these grounds being used for burial. The tribe also took offense with what was said by the medium, a baseless assumption that a spirit of their dead would commit itself to evil, which they said would not happen.

Either way, the Warrens maintained that the Lutz's accounts were real and that the haunting was the result of a dark history on the land. The evidence, both for and against the haunting stories has been debated over and over ever since. The haunting of Amityville remains one of the most famous

Ghost Stories

American cases of its nature, and the Lutz family were the last occupants to experience these terrors and speak out about them after the fact.

One of the central questions of the matter thus presents itself for explaining: If the story was a hoax, what finally drove the Lutz family to hurriedly vacate the premises less than a month after settling in? As is generally the case with sensitive stories like this, the whole and absolute truth will almost certainly remain an enigma.

Hannah J. Tidy

Chapter -16

Hauntings - Overtoun Bridge

Gateway Between Worlds

We have gone from a haunted painting to a haunted hotel, and now we cross over to something entirely unique – a haunted bridge. The Overtoun Bridge is located in the western part of Dunbartonshire in Scotland. It is situated on the estate that was formerly called Overtoun Farm before the White family purchased the land and built their mansion there. The house was erected in the 1860s, and it was soon apparent that a bridge was needed to connect the estate to its neighboring property for easier access. Hence, Overtoun Bridge was constructed in 1895.

Unlike some of the other places, we have talked about, the intriguing history of Overtoun Bridge is in no way connected to any one person. Rather unbeknownst to all at that time, Overtoun Bridge just so happened to be built on a very sacred place. The place I am talking about is known by many names across different cultures but is most commonly referred to in Gaelic culture as a "thin place." A thin place is a spot in the world in which the physical world and the spiritual world meet. It is a portal of sorts that allows spiritual beings to pass in and out of the real world. In Irish mythology, a 'thin place' is commonly found in the presence of water. The waterfall and the gushing stream that flows under the bridge certainly lend credence to this belief.

The most curious fact of the bridge, though, and the reason for its notoriety, is that at least once a year, a dog jumps off the bridge and plummets to its suicidal death.

Studies have been made into why exactly dogs are doing this in alarming numbers. While only approximately one dog per year has died since the 1960s, over 600 dogs have mysteriously taken the leap. These numbers are simply too staggering to be disregarded. Scientifically speaking, some have tried to explain these occurrences as due to an odd scent that is present at the bridge. The theory presented was

Ghost Stories

that the smell led the dogs to chase after the source causing them to leap off the bridge onto the rocky shoals beneath. But no one has been able to prove that such a scent is present.

The presence of a 'thin place' certainly would answer the question as to why dogs are doing this. I am sure you have heard about dogs that are able to sense the spiritual world. There are too many accounts to mention of dogs that have protected their masters from some unseen danger or comforted people who have recently lost loved ones by being very empathetic and consoling. Apparently, dogs have an understanding and a keen sense of seeing something that humans just don't have the ability to see with the naked eye. In fact, there is an entire show dedicated to these occurrences on the Animal Planet, entitled *The Haunted*.

When dogs come to Overtoun bridge, they must sense the presence of spirits, as the two worlds collide, and whether joy or madness drives them over the edge, who can tell? There is also a possibility that the supernatural pull on the dogs to do this is stronger at certain times of the year. One Celtic holiday, for example, is called Samhain and is

Hannah J. Tidy

described as a limited period when the physical and spiritual worlds come closer together. Our modern day Halloween has some origins in this ancient festival. A study has not yet been conducted into the timing of dog suicides on the bridge, but it might be well worth the effort.

In addition, another tragic event that transpired at the bridge also contributes towards its haunted state. In 1994 the bridge was the site of a ghastly crime. A couple named Kevin and Eileen Moy were visiting the place along with their baby boy Eoghan. Little did the wife know that her husband was about to commit a heinous act. According to the Scotland Herald, "As they stood at Overtoun Bridge near a Dumbarton beauty spot, Moy suddenly dropped the baby to the wooded banks of a river 42 feet below and then tried to throw himself over, but was dragged back by his screaming wife. Bystanders scrambled down the steep banks, where Eoghan lay fatally injured. He died in the hospital the next day."

Moy later stated that he believed that he was the Anti-Christ and that his son was Satan. In order to save the world from all the evil they would do, he had to kill his son and himself.

Ghost Stories

Whether he strongly felt the presence of the other world and was actually trying to send his son back through the portal, no one can tell. Either way, the child's death, and the man's attempted suicide are just one more connection between the bridge and the spiritual world.

Overtoun Bridge is not the only 'thin place' in the world. They exist all over the globe. For example, Aokigahara, also known as the Suicide Forest in Japan, is another one of these mysterious places, where around 100 suicides occur every year. Perhaps, in places like these, people feel the connection to the other world and cannot help but be drawn to it. Of course, you are free to visit places like these, but beware that their power may just come over you to do something that you will forever regret or pay for with your life.

Hannah J. Tidy

Ghost Stories

Chapter -17
Paranormal - Jeffrey Dahmer
Shape Shifting

We have now taken the time to look at some real life ghost stories and haunted places. It's time to move on and explore events that may seem even more bizarre - the paranormal. The Merriam-Webster Dictionary defines paranormal as something that is "very strange and not able to be explained by what scientists know about nature and the world." With the popularity of shows like *The X-Files* and *Ghost Hunters*, paranormal happenings have stepped into the spotlight. Did you know that many of the episodes of *The X-Files* are based on real life events? The man we will talk about in this chapter is the subject matter of an episode entitled *Irresistible*, the thirteenth episode of the second season of the show. The

173

man named Donnie Pfaster in the show is loosely based on the real serial killer Jeffrey Dahmer.

Jeffrey Dahmer grew up as the older of two brothers in a suburb of Milwaukee in Wisconsin. His childhood was not overly horrendous, but it was plagued by a constant fighting between his parents and the illness of his mother. He was a quiet boy, but managed to do fairly well in school and had a few friends. Early on, some oddities were noted about him. He took to collecting dead bugs and animals, and sometimes his friends would help him pick up road kill. As a young and curious boy, the behavior didn't seem very odd. However, this would only be the beginning of his fascination with death.

Things quickly went downhill as he approached Junior High. Even at the tender age of 14, he began to develop a drinking problem, and this alcoholic reputation at school caused him to become an outcast. It was during this time that Dahmer discovered that he had homosexual longings. He found himself daydreaming about relationships with other men. Even this early, Dahmer, with a keen interest in dissection, admitted that he felt the need to have complete dominance

Ghost Stories

over his sexual partner. At the age of 16, he planned the attack on a jogger that he found attractive, but was not able to go through with it, as the jogger wasn't out on the day that Dahmer lay in wait.

Things at home weren't getting any better, either. The year of his graduation from high school, his parents separated. The suddenly empty family house then became the opportune staging ground for Dahmer's first murder. He was 18. He brought a hitchhiker home, killed him, and then dissected and buried his body after sexually gratifying himself on the naked corpse. After graduation, he enlisted in the army, delaying his steps towards becoming a serial killer for nine more years. Even though he never killed anyone during his enlistment, a fellow officer did report being repeatedly raped by him.

When Dahmer returned from the army, he was sent to live with his grandmother, who resided in the same area that Dahmer grew up in. At first, things seemed to go well, and he even attended church with her and did chores. However, this didn't last long. After being propositioned by a man while reading in a library, his old desires resurfaced, and he

175

Hannah J. Tidy

once again started to actively search out sexual encounters. One thing led to another, and Dahmer once more ended up killing one of his partners. This first killing was not purposeful. Dahmer reports that he woke up the next day after a night of mutual passion with another man, but found him lying dead in bed next to him, with his chest crushed and blood everywhere. Dahmer claims that he has no recollection of actually committing this crime, but it led to an increased appetite for killings.

In total, Dahmer ended up committing 17 murders. Each death became more and more violent. He kept the skulls of his victims and even resorted to cannibalism. He ate all kinds of body parts of his victims and was even known to serve human flesh to unsuspecting people. This later earned him the nickname of the "Milwaukee Cannibal." At one point he became fascinated with the idea of a sex slave. He tried to lobotomize several of his victims in order to keep them enslaved permanently, but he never succeeded, and his victims always died. When Dahmer was finally caught, he was in the process of building an altar to himself out of the bones of the victims. When police arrested him, they found several skulls and other bones in the refrigerator, as well as

Ghost Stories

other preserved body parts that had been kept as trophies of his past killings.

Jeffrey Dahmer readily admitted to all the murders he was charged with and was imprisoned to serve 16 life sentences. Ironically, Dahmer didn't last very long in prison. He was beaten and killed by another inmate, cutting his life sentence short.

But what does all this have to do with the paranormal? It doesn't seem like Dahmer's story could get any wilder, but it does. One of Dahmer's hostages survived, and the tales he told about his tormentor are truly terrifying. He describes that Dahmer would change his form and turn into a hideous demon-like creature.

Shapeshifting has been part of legend and myth for millennia. Many old fairy tales talk about characters that can change their image back and forth into that of animals. This is usually done with the help of a deity. In Dahmer's case, the shapeshifting might be more complicated than that. The fact that the form he took was that of a demon begs the question, was Dahmer possessed?

Hannah J. Tidy

The idea of possession has been around for as long as we have had history. Perfectly ordinary people are all of a sudden overcome by an evil spirit, which forces them to do truly hideous acts. If Dahmer were indeed possessed, this would certainly explain how a normal, healthy boy could grow up and be capable of all the unspeakable horrors of his crimes.

But can possession be proven? That conundrum is the reason why debates on the veracity of paranormal events go on and on. But, certainly, for anyone who has had first-hand experience with such horrors and lived to tell the tale, it is more than real. When faced with such a credible source, we are left with only one option – to believe!

Chapter -18

Paranormal – Cannock Chase

The Black-Eyed Children

Cannock Chase is an authentic piece of pristine English land, located in the Staffordshire County, encompassing some thirty square miles. This area includes anything from forests, over large open fields, to old mines. Apart from boasting beautiful, natural scenery, Cannock Chase is also home to a long history of paranormal encounters, spanning across centuries. It is one of the hottest spots for supernatural activity in the UK.

People, since as far back as the 1800s, have reported a wide range of unexplained experiences, sightings, and confrontations. Over the years, some of the most prominent phenomena have included the notorious British big cats, which are reportedly mysterious felines about the size of a panther, certainly not indigenous to Britain. Others have reported their own versions of the most famous among the mysteries of the world, such as Bigfoot, UFOs, and even werewolves.

However, there is one particular legend, touched upon by quite a few witnesses over the last few decades, which may be the most disturbing of them all, primarily because it has a solid story behind it. With an uptick in activity during the 1980s, hikers and other wanderers have been reporting bone-chilling sightings and direct encounters with odd little children who apparently stalk the area of and around Cannock, especially the parts that are wooded. The accounts usually involve a small girl in a pale dress with bottomless, black eyes. At other times, multiple children would be reported as part of a single incident. More often than not, the encounters are also followed by different sounds, such as giggling, children asking for help, or outright screaming.

Some of those who are interested in the case, professional paranormal investigators or just curious individuals, have

Ghost Stories

suggested that these sightings may be connected to a particularly dark chapter in Cannock Chase's history.

In the 1960s, a series of abductions and murders was committed against little girls in the area. The horror began in 1964, when a cyclist, barely clenching onto her life, found a nine-year-old girl. The child had been raped, strangled, and left to die, which luckily didn't happen thanks to the passerby. A little over a year later, two girls aged only five and six, who had been missing for some time, were found dead in a ditch in Cannock Chase. Already in summer of 1967, another seven-year-old was found abused and murdered not too far away from where the previous two girls were disposed of.

The murders had a lot in common, such as that a stranger prior to disappearing lured all the girls into a car. Things soon took a turn when one girl got away from the abductor, and police began to connect the dots thanks to a witness of the attempted kidnapping. After one of the most large-scale criminal investigations and manhunts in UK's history, the police apprehended one Raymond Morris. He was charged with one of the murders, safely assumed as the perpetrator in the rest of the crimes, and locked up for life, remaining so until he died in March of 2014.

Roughly a decade after this tragic episode was when sightings of the aforementioned apparitions began. It's believed by many that it is the trapped spirits of these poor children that haunt Cannock Chase to this day, lost in the woods.

Lee Brickley, a paranormal investigator and an author, who is one of the researchers who scoured this area for all kinds of paranormal reports over the years, wrote of an encounter that his aunt had in 1982. As she had told him, it was summer of said year, and she found herself spending a day outdoors with her friend in Cannock, enjoying the nature.

At some point in the early evening hours, she thought she heard the voice of what sounded like a frightened girl calling for help from somewhere nearby. She decided to investigate just in case, trying to determine where exactly the calls were coming from. Her search led her to a simple dirt road nearby, where she immediately and clearly saw a little girl running up the road, calling for help. She went after the girl but found it impossible to catch up to her. Eventually, she

Ghost Stories

tripped, fell, and sustained a somewhat serious injury on her toe. This fall, the fact that the girl was heading into a particularly thickly wooded area and the descending darkness led her to abandon her pursuit.

After she visited the hospital next day and told the story at home, the others told her to report the incident to the police, just to be safe. Lee's aunt said that the police came the next morning to inquire about what she had seen, since this was a possible case of a missing child, though no such reports had been submitted to them at that time. It's said that the police searched the same area soon enough, but found no trace of the girl, and no report of a missing child ever came.

Rather interesting is the sudden resurgence of the sightings around 2014 because it coincides with the death of Raymond, the killer in prison. Around this time, some publications of considerable circulation in the UK began writing about increasing numbers of reports from Cannock, signaling a possible return of the ghostly children.

Soon enough, as he was known as an investigator of the Cannock Chase area, Lee Brickley began receiving reports from multiple people, mostly via email. Such was one message he was sent by an unnamed individual, who spoke of a frightful walk he took with his wife and family dog in September. The man alleged that an unnerving sound of giggling could be heard as he and his wife entered the woods. Trying to identify the source of the chuckles, the couple looked around and suddenly was confronted by a very young girl with eyes as black as coal, staring straight at them. The source said the girl stood there, in front of the frozen couple, and just observed them for a short while before she slipped into the thick, overgrown part of the woods. The witness said that he denied his wife's wish to follow the child, at which point they left.

Another email Brickley received from a woman under the name of Mrs. Kelly also piqued his interest greatly. As her story went, the woman was taking a leisurely stroll with her daughter in Birches Valley, which was interrupted by a pronounced scream from somewhere in the vicinity. She took her daughter and rushed to locate what she perceived as a child in need of help. They couldn't find anybody, but upon stopping for a quick break and then turning, Mrs. Kelly quite clearly observed a small girl, whom she judged to be around ten. The child was holding her hands over her eyes.

Ghost Stories

When the woman inquired if it was her who had been screaming and whether she was okay, the girl lowered her arms and pierced the woman with a horrifying gaze from two entirely black, soulless eyes. Petrified, Mrs. Kelly took hold of her daughter, only to notice that the strange child had vanished right then and there.

Despite the fact that the existence of the paranormal and the investigation thereof are Lee Brickley's calling, he did say that he maintains a healthy dose of skepticism toward the reports he receives, although he does take them seriously. He has said in an interview that there is always a possibility that the witnesses were hallucinating at the time of their alleged encounters. Essentially, he feels this way because he is certain that the eyewitnesses he got in contact with are genuine.

What about evidence of the black-eyed girls, then? There have been some photos and pieces of video footage captured over time, but some are more veracious than others. For instance, there was a photo released in 2014, from a woman called Melissa Mason, which shows two of her kids climbing a tree and what appears to be a ghost of a child on the right

185

side of the picture. It certainly does look like a ghost, but such an effect can easily be fabricated nowadays, and it's unsafe to assume that this was anything but a Halloween prank.

On the other hand, a team of paranormal investigators called the Haunted Finders captured a certain video in 2015, which they claim shows a silhouette of one of the child ghosts. Tom Buckmaster, the ghost buster who recorded the footage, explained that, to him, it looked as though he could see the figure's legs moving as it walks through the woods. This may be best left to the eye of the beholder to decide, but there are a few aspects of the footage that are interesting.

Firstly, the video, which was a result of some six hours of searching through the woods, does appear to be entirely genuine, with no signs of tampering. The footage was made in the almost absolute darkness of the Cannock Chase woods, with what appears to be the camera's light illuminating the trees only mere feet within view, beyond which everything is pitch-black. Then, a pale figure can be seen slipping past further ahead in the woods, just beyond the light's range. The silhouette indeed appears to be moving

Ghost Stories

as it quickly disappears into the dark. Within the messages in the video, the team raises the issue, and rightfully so, of how exactly the mysterious shape can be seen so distinctly in the enveloping darkness. It does appear that, as they said, it has its own light source.

While what people say may be the source of these ghosts is a verifiable story that we have covered, the allegations remain largely inconclusive. It serves the story's veracity that many of the accounts, including older ones, share the same details about the appearance and behavior of the black-eyed ghosts. Another thing to consider is that Cannock Chase is not the only place where these reports have emerged. The United States has seen its own share of encounters with the black-eyed apparitions. Either way, the phenomenon is gaining popularity, and the diligent paranormal investigators are hard at work. These circumstances are always bound to produce more evidence sooner than later.

Hannah J. Tidy

Ghost Stories

Chapter -19

Paranormal – Mount Washington Hotel

The Carolyn Stickney EVP

Murky old photos, spoken testimonies, and age-old legends are, of course, not the only form of evidence that you can come across if you search for the paranormal phenomena or ghosts. Sometimes, something much more concrete comes along and leaves even the firmest of skeptics scratching their heads. That is exactly what we have on our hands in this incredible, bewildering story.

In case it needs explanation, EVP stands for Electronic Voice Phenomena. Ghost hunters, paranormal investigators, and other enthusiasts sometimes use this method in locations purported as being haunted or host to a paranormal activity

Hannah J. Tidy

of any kind. It involves recording sounds with a variety of devices, and performing a deep analysis of the audio after the fact, so as to search for any possible peculiarities. Essentially, EVPs are recordings thought to contain sounds made by actual ghosts and other paranormal forces. Every now and then, something quite fascinating is picked up by investigators.

Such is the case of Princess Carolyn Stickney and her supposed haunting of the Mount Washington Hotel, although "haunting" may not be the most suitable word for what has been observed. This is because she doesn't seem to be a malicious ghost, and the word "haunting" often carries with it a negative connotation. Most of the strange occurrences reported at the hotel usually boil down to flickering lights, alleged appearances of the ghost, unexplained sounds, smaller objects disappearing and the like. What she does seem to be, however, is one of the most convincing possible ghosts ever documented. And this is because of one particular case involving an EVP, which we will cover soon enough.

Ghost Stories

The Mount Washington Hotel was masterminded by a wealthy railroad industrialist by the name of Joseph Stickney in 1900, in New Hampshire. Around two years and a fortune later, the hotel was officially opened in 1902. Joseph had put a lot of money and effort into the construction of this masterpiece but passed away only a year after it was opened. Carolyn, the succeeding owner of the hotel, made some contributions of her own to the hotel over the next decade, building a new floor between the hotel's towers, a private dining room for her inner circle, and a chapel in memory of Joseph. She also had a big balcony installed, overlooking the primary dining room of the hotel, from where she could observe the guests. There have been reports, over the years, of her apparition showing up on this balcony in particular.

After a while, she remarried a French prince, which is the reason she was, and is often referred to, as Princess Carolyn, or simply Princess. She spent a certain time in France with her royal husband but returned to spend her last days in the hotel and the scenery she enjoyed after her second husband died as well. She had her own private apartment, now Room 314, and she had her personal bed brought in because she felt uncomfortable sleeping in any other. This bed is in the room to this day. As you would expect, this particular room is something of a hotspot for paranormal activity. There have been numerous reports of strange happenings in there, including flickering lights and unusual noises, and one report from a visiting couple, of a woman sitting on the bed, fixing her hair.

Reports of paranormal activity by hotel employees began not too long after Carolyn's death in 1936. Her apparition was reportedly seen in her favorite hotel spots quite a few times, and a mysterious figure would show up in photographs of the staff after they developed them. This was also the time when people at the hotel already began talking about lights shutting on and off by themselves, and even bathtubs being mysteriously filled up.

However, it was in February of 2008 when the most impressive paranormal evidence cropped up. Jason and Grant, two investigators from The Atlantic Paranormal Society (TAPS), decided to investigate the stories at the hotel. They were working as part of their "Ghost Hunters" show on Syfy. They conducted a thorough investigation of

Ghost Stories

the Mt. Washington Hotel, and they focused especially on the infamous Room 314. The two Ghost Hunters confirmed hearing and recorded mysterious steps throughout the hotel, for which they couldn't identify the source.

However, this was child's play compared to what they caught on tape in the Princess' old quarters in Room 314. It was here where they tried to elicit paranormal activity and establish contact with the supposed ghost by asking her questions. No one could have predicted the mysterious outcome as the exclusively male crew started getting their answers, in a female voice. The voice was not perfectly clear but it was almost entirely audible and what was said could be discerned with almost complete confidence.

At first, in the footage featured on the show, the men are seen standing in and observing the room, apparently commenting on the interior and discussing the case. In the midst of them talking, the recording devices picked up what appeared to be a female voice saying something very quickly and then again as they are discussing the Princess' old bed. After that, the investigators attempted to talk to the ghost directly. One of the men quietly asked, "Princess, are you in here?" The same, muffled voice, sounding as if it was coming from under the water, responded in a barely audible manner. It did seem to appear that she said, "Hello. Is there someone there?" The man repeated his question and asked her to confirm that she was in the room. Things get creepy at this point, as she responds once again, this time more clearly. Most would agree that she said, "Of course I'm in here. Where are you?" Still, the voice was not entirely audible, but it was definitely improving.

The team tried to get her to give a physical sign by moving an object or doing something of the sort. All of their questions were met with the same answer, though. "Of course I'm in here. Where are you?" she kept asking.

The audio recording and video footage were, of course, featured on the Ghost Hunters episode, but are also available on the internet for anybody to see. In the episode, the Ghost Hunters were seen showing their audio recordings to the head of security at the hotel, Fred Hollis, and filming his reaction. It took no incentives from anybody to see how genuinely the man immediately reacted at the very first moment when the female voice briefly makes herself known.

He said that he could clearly understand what was being said, and his reaction was, in my opinion, that of genuine but controlled fascination. Everybody who watches the footage can judge for themselves, though.

Hollis went on to explain that he had his own strange experiences at the hotel in the past, such as mysterious sounds. These peculiar incidents he witnessed were usually very subtle, just enough to arouse suspicion, but not enough for a rational man to draw a definite conclusion from. At the times when his "encounters" happened, he was unsure of what he heard, if anything at all, so he didn't pay that much mind to any of it. However, the recordings presented to him by the Ghost Hunters crew, he said, were absolutely in line with his past experiences. He now had confirmation that he had indeed been hearing mysterious sounds around the hotel.

What some may find particularly fascinating about this case is that the ghost itself is quite different from what you would usually expect, based on most of the stories of hauntings in popular culture. Princess Carolyn's life wasn't that of tragedy, and neither was her death. She lived a fulfilled life,

Hannah J. Tidy

ran the hotel until her very end, and passed away naturally in a place she loved. Could this be the reason that her supposed ghost actually appears to be pleasant, and could it be possible for a trapped soul wandering the physical world, to even be friendly? This is kind of interesting to ponder over if we assume that this was, in fact, the ghost of Carolyn.

Once one hears the exchange with the ghostly voice, they might also get the sense that whoever or whatever it is on tape may be in a spiritual state totally opposite to that which we would expect in a ghost. It's almost as if the recording lets us see into the "psyche" of a ghost. In particular, more so than just being friendly, Carolyn, perhaps, comes across as being somewhat confused and lost. Most of us would usually think of a ghost as a haunting presence, often malicious and even dangerous, that is in perfect control over its reality, while we are the ones who are confused, petrified, and helpless.

Although hearing a ghostly voice talk back to you in a haunted place would be terrifying and make anybody's hair stand up, once you think about this recording, things take on a whole new light. The way that the Princess keeps asking if someone is there and simply saying hello, gives us the impression of someone who doesn't know what exactly is going on. She doesn't want to throw things around, cut the phone lines, terrify anybody, or make the walls bleed. Instead, she simply appears to be trying to establish communication, just like the Ghost Hunters were doing. And if she actually responded with, "Of course I'm here," then that implies that in her world or plane of existence, there is no doubt as to what she is and what she's doing. It's almost as if the Ghost Hunters themselves are the intruders, disturbing her peace, and not the other way around. Maybe the living souls that visit the hotel appear as ghosts to Carolyn, leaving her just as confused as we would be upon seeing or hearing an apparition.

We'd never think that we would be the ones who have to explain ourselves if we ran into a ghost. Apart from her being somewhat perplexed by the investigators' questioning of her presence, the rest of the exchange still implies a dose of confusion from the ghost's point-of-view.

There is a wide array of interesting posts, on forums and other places on the internet, from people giving their

Hannah J. Tidy

thoughts and theories as to what is going on. Some suggest that this exchange is proof that we who are the living and those who have departed exist simultaneously in two parallel realms of existence. Sometimes, these realms flow into each other in something of an inter-dimensional glitch, if you will. This overlap makes ghosts of those who have died stumble into our realm by accident, resulting in all kinds of paranormal phenomena for the witnesses. On the other hand, it could be that we can accidentally slip into the spiritual world just the same. Perhaps ghosts are not even aware of their death, and they just continue living as if nothing happened, without even knowing that they have transcended into a new reality, in what appears to be their regular life. Could it be, then, that if a living, mortal soul was to wander beyond their three-dimensional world, those who occupy the beyond might be just as shocked as we are when we perceive the supposed ghosts?

Furthermore, the spirit of the late Carolyn may be trapped in time in a way that we can't even fathom, where it flows in a non-linear way or just freezes completely. Her perception of time may be entirely different to that of ours, leading to a lot of confusion.

Ghost Stories

Whatever the case may be, and whether or not the recordings are valid proof of paranormal activity, we can hardly draw any definitive conclusions, even after watching the episode and hearing the uncanny recording for ourselves. There are a few things we can do, though. We can speculate on what this may or may not prove, and what it tells us about the paranormal. Alternatively, we can simply stay at the Mount Washington Hotel, which continues to be a prosperous institution to this day. They offer an authentic vintage experience of luxury and incredible scenery, as well as the possibility to have your own paranormal encounter. After all, Carolyn's shenanigans, as well as other reported ghostly activity, are not kept secret and the hotel doesn't try to hide this peculiar quirk in their luxury accommodation.

Hannah J. Tidy

Chapter -20

Paranormal – The Goldfield Hotel

The Clearest EVP Ever Recorded?

There have been numerous alleged Electronic Voice Phenomena over the years, and going over all of them would be quite a tedious feat. After all, a lot of the recordings of this kind are rather distorted, dim, or not particularly awe-inspiring, so it's not just about the number of purported EVPs, but also their low quality. There may be only a few EVPs that come close to the Princess of Mt. Washington Hotel, which would definitely make them worthy of investigation. The recording from the old Goldfield Hotel is one of them without a doubt, as it also has the capacity to blow your hair back. Arguably, it is even more bewildering than Princess Carolyn, especially considering some of the

Hannah J. Tidy

other stories, events, and investigative experiences in Goldfield Hotel, before and long after its closure in 1945.

The Goldfield Hotel is a dilapidated and allegedly deeply haunted building in a small, stagnating town of Goldfield in the state of Nevada. The history of this town begins in 1902 with the discovery of gold in the area, which sparked an influx of people and quickly got the town established. It wasn't long at all until the city became very active and prosperous due to the rich mining industry around it. Soon, it became the largest city in the state and was home to some 35,000 people at its peak.

However, not even a decade passed until the resources started to deplete in the mines, causing many of the townsfolk to move on and take the gold rush elsewhere. As the gold mining industry declined, the town began to devolve as well. Ultimately, all of the gold ore was used up and the town was hit by a terrible fire in the 1920s. The population decreased dramatically, amounting to some five hundred people today.

The Goldfield Hotel itself was officially opened in 1908 as quite a luxurious place, boasting four stories and a total of

Ghost Stories

154 rooms, fully equipped with the necessary utilities. The hotel became successful very quickly, mainly because it drew in guests from the upper classes, particularly those who came through looking to invest or start their own gold mining ventures.

One such man was a wealthy mining industrialist named George Winfield, who soon bought the hotel as part of his hotel entrepreneurship side-path. His investment made him quite a lot of money, adding to his already enormous wealth.

Winfield is allegedly also one of the ghosts who still haunt the historic hotel, along with a ghost of a woman called Elizabeth. According to some controversial legends, the two had known each other rather well when they were still among the living. There have been numerous reports of other ghosts wandering the building, such as those of children and at least two other people who allegedly committed suicide in the hotel. The tale of Winfield and Elizabeth, though, is particularly dark.

Elizabeth is said to have been a prostitute around the 1920s and 30s, with George Winfield as one of her regular customers. As the story goes on to suggest, misfortune

203

struck when Elizabeth found out she was pregnant and told Winfield he was the father, urging him to leave his wife and marry her instead. George tried to keep her away, giving her money to survive on her own and keep the pregnancy quiet. He was hoping to avoid complications that could harm him, as he was a prominent and influential individual in Nevada at the time. His plan didn't work for very long, however, as Elizabeth was relentless in her demands for justice and ultimately returned to him.

Things take a dark turn here, as Elizabeth is believed to have died in the 1930s in one of two ways. Some suggest she simply died at childbirth, but others have alleged that Winfield murdered her in cold blood. This didn't happen right away, however. It is said that he tied Elizabeth to a radiator in his private Room 109 at the hotel, and kept her so until she was about to give birth. He made sure she was fed and provided her with water to keep her alive. According to different versions of the story, she either died in the room when it came time to birth their child or Winfield murdered her after the fact. After that, some say, he took the baby to the basement and threw it down one of the mine shafts that the hotel was built on.

Ghost Stories

Whether or not these events transpired as the legend says they did is debated to this day, but reports of their ghosts and other paranormal activity at the hotel have been numerous, to say the least. The hotel is widely known as a haunted place, and it attracts many visitors and enthusiasts. This is also one of the reasons that efforts to renovate have stagnated for decades, as a lot of trespassing and vandalism have occurred.

Among the visitors was a crew from Ghost Adventures, who came to investigate the reports on multiple occasions. In 2008, the Ghost Adventures show organized a well-documented, videotaped investigation of the premises, which was featured later on. This was when one of the most incredible paranormal videos was made, and it's well-known among the circles interested in the paranormal. The team can be seen lurking around in the basement, looking for anything strange and recording with their cameras. They go around in the darkness, asking for any ghosts to come out if they are around. Just moments after that, a brick lifts off and flies across the room, smashing against the wall with the most terrifying noise. The situation gets hectic quickly, and the investigators scramble in the darkness. At this time, what sounds like children's voices can be heard periodically from somewhere around them. Of course, it didn't take long for the team to disappear from the premises, and this EVP was among the last things recorded during this particular excursion by the Ghost Adventures.

However, this wasn't even close to the best EVP recording obtained at the Goldfield Hotel. This shocker came some time later when the Ghost Adventures returned once again. This time, however, they had Mark and Debby Constantino with them. This couple was in the same line of work, but they were fairly skeptical of both the hotel and the footage previously presented by Ghost Adventures. As a matter of fact, the Constantinos, who were leading the investigation, brought a news crew from the KTVN with cameras, ready to capture all the evidence right on television.

Similar to the previous visit by the Ghost Adventures, the Constantinos also went around for a while, recording, asking for any sign from the ghosts, if they are present. In the piece, Debby can be seen using a sound recorder as she tries to communicate. They don't hear anything at first, and nothing is captured by the cameras. However, she then tries a

Ghost Stories

different approach. Apparently, Debby thought that perhaps they couldn't hear the EVPs with their own ears at the time, so she asked the ghost, "Can you at least tell me, in the recorder, if you did it?" referring to the incident with the brick.

Then, they played back what the recorder had picked up, and were shocked to hear a response. What resembled a female voice, responded in almost entirely clear English, "Thank you, but we've done it." The words sounded slightly cut up, and there was a little bit of static, but the recording is very difficult to argue with. But the investigators didn't stop there. They managed to engage the alleged ghost once again, using the same method.

The team asked another question and continued to inquire about the brick that was thrown. The voice could be heard responding again with, "Didn't mean to hurt anybody." This second response was even more audible than the first one. Matters of authenticity aside, the recorded, spoken word is next to irrefutable in the audio. Still, there really haven't been many claims against the recordings being fake, and there has been no evidence presented to expose the audio as anything but genuine.

Another fact perhaps worth mentioning is that the Constantino couple was found dead in an apartment in 2015, in what was ruled as a murder-suicide perpetrated by Mark in a case of domestic violence gone terribly wrong. It's unclear what exactly led to this tragedy, but the couple had a strained relationship for a while and was going through a range of other personal problems in their lives.

As for our mystery voice in the Goldfield Hotel, it remains one of those clear, understandable enigmas, as paradoxical as that is. If there truly is a spirit at work on the premises, it's also unclear if this would indeed be the restless soul of Elizabeth or someone else. Her apparition was described in reports as a sad, heart-broken lady, who hopelessly stalks the hallways in search of her child. As for Winfield, some witnesses have alleged that they would run into traces of mysterious cigar smoke that seems to emit from no natural source. They purport that this could be the residue of his spirit, as it traverses his old hotel, smoking the cigars he enjoyed in life just the same. There are problems with the

Ghost Stories

legend of these two departed, though, and inconsistencies between different versions. It is known that Winfield didn't remain the owner of the hotel until the very end. Instead, it was sold to another man not long after the town began to deteriorate. There are thus conflicting accounts of when exactly Elizabeth died, and if Winfield had even been the owner at the time it happened.

Details of such stories, which span back for decades and were spread by word of mouth mostly, can often become muddled up and result in confusion and disarray in the story. However, that isn't to say that there isn't a fine thread of truth that snakes its way through the different versions and recollections. This is especially true when there is so much strange activity, reported by so many people, who can't explain just what they experienced. Combined with the startling, documented evidence that hasn't been refuted, all of this makes for an unusual place that continues to garner much attention as people who are thirsty for answers pass through the hotel in search of the truth.

Hannah J. Tidy

Ghost Stories

Chapter -21
Paranormal - Natasha Demkina:

X-Ray Vision

Just as both evil and good exist in the physical world, the same applies to the spiritual realm. In the last twenty-six chapters we have focused on the gory and evil side of ghosts and paranormal activity, but ending on a positive note seems more beneficial. You know how after you watch a horror movie you need to watch or read something else, something light, before settling in for your restful night? Consider this the chapter that does that.

Paranormal activity in humans, while frightening, can also be quite rewarding. Stan Lee, who helped create famous comic book heroes such as The Avengers and The Amazing Spider-Man, decided to come out with a television show that broadcast the superhuman or paranormal abilities of men and women all over the world and entitled it *Stan Lee's Superhumans*. These wide-ranged paranormal abilities covered everything, from superhuman strength to superhuman mental acuity. People featured on this show include Salim Haini, known for his incredible ability to eat anything, Zamora the Torture King, who is able to skewer himself without feeling any pain whatsoever, and Miroslaw Magola, a man with telekinetic abilities.

Some of these abilities may seem more valuable than others. But imagine if you had an ability that could truly help others? Would you use your power? This is the choice that Natasha Demkina faces every day.

Ghost Stories

Natasha was born in 1987 in Saransk, Mordovia. While her life appeared to be completely normal at the start, her parents soon took notice of a special ability that set her apart, an ability that lay in her vision. One day Natasha walked into the room and became aware of her ability to see her mother's organs, as though she had x-ray vision. However, unlike with x-ray, Natasha was able to see each organ in full living color and movement. Imagine how the wealth of information generated by all the additional detail of Natasha's vision could aid doctors in the accuracy of their diagnosis. Once her mother had told others of her abilities, local residents frequently dropped by to receive prognoses from the girl with the unusual ability.

Natasha spent a lot of time in Russia helping doctors at the children's hospital in Saransk with quite a bit of success. Among her accurate 'readings,' Natasha was able to see the precise location of an ulcer in one of the doctor's stomach. She was also able to differentiate benign cysts from the cancerous material. Word about her unique gift inevitably spread around the world, and she was soon invited to England, the United States, and then Japan, to talk about and prove her abilities. The test in New York City, however,

213

did not put Natasha in a good light. Her success rate only seemed to be at a little under 60%. Because of these results, the scientific world in the United States, as well as many other countries, felt that Natasha had been legitimately discredited. It appeared to the critics that she was merely a psychic, a good one at that, who was able to 'read' people in order to diagnose them.

Meanwhile, other experts attempted to discredit the criticisms. The test in Tokyo, Japan, went much smoother than the test administered in the United States, finally making a valid case for the authenticity of her skills. As Natasha's superhuman ability is only in her vision, and not in her capacity to diagnose, she is currently studying medicine at Semashkow's Moscow Medical University. Hopefully, this will help her fine tune her skills and save many lives in the future.

There you have it! We have gone through some pretty intriguing, if not gruesome and horrifying true-to-life events. While real mysteries often cannot be logically explained, sometimes we just have to accept it. Not all of the paranormal is evil, and not all evil acts stem from the

Ghost Stories

paranormal. Faced with the known facts, it is within ourselves to choose what to believe in, and what we deny.

Hannah J. Tidy

Conclusion

I hope you have enjoyed these baffling and shocking stories that dealt with ghosts, hauntings, and paranormal activities around the world. There are one too many hard-to-believe stories that will continually challenge us to keep an open mind. Being aware, though, may one day, save your soul.

Most of the events presented above begin and end with no seeming sense of logic.

While these stories may seem improbable, the known evidence will make you wonder... what if? Legends and myths have come to be for a reason. And each story may have the tiniest truth to it. But the truth, logical or fanatical, will eventually reveal itself. Understanding this concept may help us accept that which is unacceptable.

The unsettled spirits make no distinction with whom they torment. All we can do is believe.

While most creepy stories begin and end with mysteries, one thing is positive...

Understanding these stories will also help you better understand the legends and myths that pervade so many cultures in the world. Remember that almost every story has a seed of truth in it - no matter how far - fetched it may seem.

Ghosts and spirits do not discriminate in their activity by class, or area of the world, even though some places seem to have more paranormal activity than others. People from all walks of life and all social classes have had their run-ins with hauntings, ghostly apparitions, and humans with paranormal abilities. From the wealthiest people, such as Sarah Winchester, to the most neglected soul such as Richard Ramirez, all are connected with the spiritual world

Ghost Stories

and are equally susceptible to hauntings and other ghostly activities.

Chances are you will have your own personal run-in at some point in your life. Just as groups exist for those who believe in extraterrestrial life, you can also find a support group if you end up dealing with a disturbing spiritual experience. Just remember, you are not alone.

Hannah J. Tidy

Works Cited

Barrington, George. "An Account of a Voyage to New South Wales." *Sherwood, Neely & Jones, London.* 1810.

BBC. "The eBay Haunted Painting." *BBC.* July 2002. Web. 9 May 2016.

Dean, Bryan. Brewer, Graham Lee. Medley, Robert. "Mother believes religious cult is responsible for Oklahoma family's disappearance." *The Oklahoman.* 19 November 2013. Web. 9 May 2016.

Merriam-Webster. "Paranormal." *Merriam-Webster Learner's Dictionary.* 2016. Web. 9 May 2016.

Stoneham, William. "The Hands Resist Him." *Stoneham Studios.* 2015. Web. 9 May 2016.

The Scotland Herald. "Father who threw 'devil' baby from bridge sent to Carstairs." *Herald Scotland.* 31 January 1995. Web. 9 May 2016.

Ghost Stories

About The Author

Hannah J. Tidy is a non-fiction writer who writes about true events on ghost and horror stories. She was born in the beautiful city of Riverside, CA, in the United states. She attended University of Riverside where she got her Bachelor's degree in Arts. Hannah has a passion for writing dating back to her elementary, and as such, her creativity and ability to put words into perfect use makes her a prolific writer. Being a skeptic, she didn't believe to much in the ghost but that quickly changed after she had a Horrifying experience herself. She is now passionate about reporting true ghost and horror stories.

Having her readers in mind when writing, she focuses on putting stories that will not only scare her readers, but also gives them a piece or two to think about. Her books are always interesting, fascinating, and engaging making them a joy to read and has gained love by her readers.

When she is not writing, she enjoys spending time with her family and friends as well as biking and Traveling.

Thank you for reading my book, I'd love to hear your opinion about my book. In the world of book publishing, there are few things more valuable than honest reviews from a wide variety of readers.

Your review will help other readers find out whether my book is for them. It will also help me reach more readers by increasing the visibility of my book.

You can leave your review **here** (the link takes you directly to the review form on Amazon)

Check Out my other books

Horror Stories

Terrifyingly REAL Stories of true horror & Chilling- Murders

Hannah J. Tidy

Chapter 1:

The Hinterkaifeck Farm

A quiet and serene alpine forest lends itself to one of the most gruesome murders of all time. In 1922, just inside the borders of the German town of Bavaria, an unassuming farm fell victim to what some believe to have been the work of the Devil or that of a demon. The farm was called Hinterkaifeck Farmstead, about an hour outside of Munich, Germany. The family who lived there were the Gruebers: Andreas, husband to Cazilia, and father to Viktoria. Viktoria was widowed and lived with her mother and father along with her two children, Cazilia (7 years old) and Josef (2 years old).

Hannah J. Tidy

The family was not particularly liked among the townspeople. Although the family lived a considerable distance outside of town, they were well known by the villagers as being reclusive, sullen and mostly kept to themselves. Andreas was known for regularly beating his wife, Cazilia, as well as being brutal to his own children. Viktoria is the only surviving child of her father's temper as none of her siblings survived the beatings. Josef, Viktoria's son, was believed to be the incestuous daughter of Viktoria and Andreas, her father. Andreas was obsessed with Viktoria and forbade her to even get remarried. She was well thought of, as much as many members of this family could be, by townsfolk. Viktoria often attended church and sang in the church choir.

One day, the Grueber's maid quit her job and requested to leave almost immediately. The maid, Maria, stated that she no longer wanted to work in the home because of strange sounds and voices that she had heard, as well as footsteps echoing from the vacant attic. Maria was convinced that the home was haunted and that she was not safe if she stayed and wished not to remain a second longer. Witnesses stated that Maria was pale and emaciated when she left, looking as

Ghost Stories

if she had seen or heard tales of horror. The Gruebers did not take Maria seriously and rather believed her to be mentally disturbed.

About six months later, another strange and mysterious occurrence ensued. Andreas was outside walking in the front yard near the woods and discovered odd shaped footsteps in the snow. He followed these footsteps until he reached the house where they led to the front door. The footsteps stopped right outside the front door, where the snow had been cleared away from the walkway. Andreas was concerned because he looked all over the property and did not find any other footsteps leading from the house back out to the forest. He thought perhaps, an intruder was inside the house, someone who had come walking through the woods on this cold night. However, Andreas searched and searched all over the house but did not find anyone and nothing was out of place or missing. The Grueber's carried on with their night, unable to figure out where the footsteps might have come from.

To check out the rest of (Horror Stories) on Amazon.

Hannah J. Tidy

Or go to:

http://www.nightterrorpublishing.com/product/horror-stories/

To receive a discount

Made in the USA
Lexington, KY
16 August 2017